CONSCIOUS EVOLUTION:

A LOVE STORY

CONSCIOUS EVOLUTION: A LOVE STORY

HEALING THE GLOBAL INTIMACY DISORDER BY JOINING GENIUS

HONORING THE LIFE OF BARBARA MARX HUBBARD

• • •

From Conscious Evolution 1.0 to Conscious Evolution 2.0

One Mountain, Many Paths: Oral Essays
Volume Fourteen

DR. MARC GAFNI AND
BARBARA MARX HUBBARD

Author: Marc Gafni and Barbara Marx Hubbard
Title: Conscious Evolution: A Love Story
From Conscious Evolution 1.0 to Conscious Evolution 2.0

Identifiers: ISBN 979-8-88834-080-6 (electronic)
ISBN 979-8-88834-079-0 (paperback)

Edited by Timothy Paul Aryeh, Talya Bloom, and Rachel Keune

World Philosophy and Religion Press, St. Johnsbury, VT
in conjunction with

IP Integral Publishers

https://worldphilosophyandreligion.org

JOIN THE REVOLUTION!

CONTENTS

EDITORIAL NOTE ABOUT AUTHORSHIP, EDITING, AND
    THE RADICAL CONTEXT FOR THIS SERIES   XIII

LOVE OR DIE: LOCATING OURSELVES   XXV

ABOUT THIS VOLUME   XLII

CHAPTER 1   BARBARA'S MEMORIAL IN
                      EVOLUTIONARY CHURCH

Beloved Barbara   1

Before Prayer   6

Eulogy for Barbara   10

Evolutionary Love Code: Love Is a Perception   11

Barbara Was the Good News   13

I Am Evolution in Person   14

I Am Getting Newer   15

If You Want to Know the Essence of Barbara   17

She Charmed Us   18

Joining Genes to Joining Genius   20

There May Be a Time, but This Is Not That Day   23

We Go to Prayer   25

CHAPTER 2   **RESURRECTION AND RENEWAL: RECLAIMING LOVE IN EVOLUTIONARY CHURCH**

Barbara, You Are Alive Here in Church With Us   29

Not Just *Tat Tvam Asi* or the Infinity of Power, God Is Also the
    Infinity of Intimacy   34

The Infinity of Intimacy Carries Us in Every Second   35

Evolutionary Love Code: There Is No Eros Without Gnosis   37

Reality Moves Towards Resurrection   40

We Are *Homo Amor* Moving Towards Resurrection   41

CHAPTER 3   **MORE THAN CONFESSING YOUR SINS, YOU MUST CONFESS YOUR GREATNESS**

Reality Is a Set of Habits   43

Our Intention Is to Participate in the Evolution of Love   44

The World Needs a Story About the Evolutionary Love That
    Animates Everything   47

God Is the Infinity of Intimacy Into Whose Arms I Fall in
    Every Moment   48

Barbara Marx Hubbard Is With Us in the Continuity
    of Consciousness   50

Evolutionary Love Code: To Love God Is to Know God   50

Our Clarified Heart's Desire Becomes Part of the Field of Desire   54

CHAPTER 4   **AWAKENING HOMO AMOR: PARTICIPATING IN THE EVOLUTION OF LOVE**

Welcoming Barbara	59
The Global Intimacy Disorder: We Don't Have a Shared Story	60
Evolutionary Love Code: Your Deepest Heart's Desire Is the Source of Great Joy	62
What Is *Homo Amor*?	64
Who Is *Homo Amor Universalis*?	66
Homo Amor Universalis: A New Understanding of All Our Dimensions	67
Homo Amor Is Our Response to the Second Shock of Existence	68
The Inner Experience of *Homo Amor Universalis* Is That Reality Is Literally 50/50	69
What Does Evolution Need From Me in This Next Moment?	71

CHAPTER 5   **A CRISIS OF TOUCH: BECOMING THE MOTHER TO EACH OTHER**

God in First Person, Second Person, and Third Person	73
All the Rivers Flow Back to the Sea	75
The Sacred Technology of Chant	77
Evolutionary Love Code: Evolution Is the Evolution of Intimacy	77
Our Intention Is to Tell the New Story	78
The One Church Is the Shared Music of All the Great Religions	80
Crisis in the World: We've Forgotten What It Means to Touch Each Other	81
The Allurement to Touch Each Other Is Fundamental to Cosmos	83
The Four-Fold Exile of Touch	84
We Have to Heal the Hug	87

CHAPTER 6   **RECLAIMING & EVOLVING INTIMACY: EVERYONE'S IN THE CIRCLE**

I Am Ready to Play a Larger Game, to Participate in the
Evolution of Love   89

Homo Amor Reunites Love and Knowledge   90

We Pray to the Intimate Face of the Evolutionary Impulse   92

Avengers Endgame: We All Have a Unique Self Superpower   93

Evolutionary Love Code: Birthing New Structures of Intimacy   94

We Unleash New Synergies in the World   95

Avengers Endgame: I'm Not Separate From the Larger Whole   96

CHAPTER 7   **OUR TOUCH QUIVERS REALITY TO NEW IDENTITY; GOD ASKS EVERYTHING OF ME**

Living My Life to the Fullest, Chapter and Verse in the Universe:
A Love Story   99

Prayer: Every Place You Fall, You Fall Into Her Arms   101

Evolutionary Love Code: There Are No Externalities   103

CHAPTER 8   **THERE ARE NO DEPLORABLES: EVERYBODY IS INSIDE THE CIRCLE**

Radical Surprise and Amazement: We Get to Participate in
the Evolution of Love!   107

There's An Ontological Pluralism in a Perennial Context   110

The New Story Is the New Physics of Reality   111

The Infinity of Power Is Also the Infinity of Intimacy   112

How Do You Practically Locate Intimacy in Your Life?   114

Opening the Circle and Letting Everyone In   115

Loving Our Way to Enlightenment   118

CHAPTER 9   **OPENING YOUR HEART IS NOT ENOUGH; NO PART OF YOU SHOULD BE LEFT OUT**

We Become the Leading Edge of Evolution   121

Prayer: Reclaiming the God That Knows Me   124

Exponentialized Desire and Exponentialized Tenderness   125

Evolutionary Love Code: Enlightenment Means There Are
    No Externalities   126

Who Have I Left Out of My Heart?   127

You Can't Love a Person If You've Left Other People Out of
    Your Heart   128

When You're in Crisis, What's New About You Is Often Left Out   130

We Are the People Telling the New Story   134

CHAPTER 10   **CONSCIOUS EVOLUTION: A LOVE STORY**

Poised at the Abyss, We Are Called to Evolution   137

We're Bringing the New Good News   138

Evolution Is the Evolution of Intimacy   140

What's the Source of All This? Where Does This Drive for
    Intimacy Come From?   141

I See You With God's Eyes   144

When I See With God's Eyes, I Can See the Next Step in the
    Evolution of Love   145

God's Perspective of Us at This Moment of Evolution   147

Find the Form of Joining Genius   149

APPENDIX: SONGS   **150**

INDEX   **154**

ABOUT THE AUTHORS   **162**

EDITORIAL NOTE ABOUT AUTHORSHIP, EDITING, AND THE RADICAL CONTEXT FOR THIS SERIES

ORAL ESSAYS FROM THE ONE MOUNTAIN, MANY PATHS WEEKLY BROADCAST

This volume is part of the Oral Essays library, a series of lightly edited, compiled transcripts of oral teachings given by Dr. Marc Gafni and the late Barbara Marx Hubbard in their weekly online broadcast, *One Mountain, Many Paths,* which they co-founded in 2017. Originally called an "Evolutionary Church," *One Mountain, Many Paths* became a key venue for the articulation of an inspired and deeply grounded new Story of Value in response to the meta-crisis. Marc and Barbara—together with Zak Stein,[1] Kristina Kincaid, Ken Wilber, Sally Kempton, Lori Galperin, Aubrey Marcus and dozens of other thought-leaders over the years—began to articulate what they call a World Philosophy and World Religion[2] as a context for our diversity.

---

1   Zak, together with Ken Wilber, has been Marc's primary intellectual partner and an initiate lineage holder in CosmoErotic Humanism.

2   This project is grounded in four core organizational frameworks: 1) The Center for World Philosophy and Religion, co-founded by Marc Gafni, Zachary Stein, Sally Kempton, and Ken Wilber, and chaired over the years by John P. Mackey, Barbara Marx Hubbard, Aubrey Marcus, Gabrielle Anwar and Shareef Malnik, Carrie Kish and Adam Bellow, and Kathleen J. Brownback. 2) The Office for the Future, chaired by Stephanie Valcke and Ivan Bossyut. 3) The World Philosophy and Religion Press, founded and chaired by Aubrey Marcus, together with Marc Gafni and Zachary Stein. 4) The Foundation for Conscious Evolution, founded by Barbara Marx Hubbard and currently chaired by Peter Fiekowsky. For a complete list of key leadership, see the Office for the Future website, www.officeforthefuture.com.

Until Barbara's passing in 2019, she and Marc transmitted teachings together as evolutionary partners and "whole mates," weaving together insights and transmissions from their decades of practice, study, teaching, and activism into a synergy of wisdom, a grounded vision for future policy across all sectors of society.

Much of the Dharma material below comes directly from Marc, so it was originally all in quotation marks—but that looked a little odd. So per his suggestion we removed them, and the reader should consider the paragraphs on the next several pages as one extended quote from him. We are joyfully grateful to Marc for the clarity of his Dharma, the elegance and "second simplicity" of this language, and the mad, Outrageous Love with which he transmits his teachings.

Barbara and Marc called the mission of *One Mountain* "a Planetary Awakening in Evolutionary Love Through Unique Self Symphonies." We are an evolutionary community with a deeply grounded, radically alive, and "post-tragic" revolutionary spirit. We are activating a new humanity and awakening as a new species: *Homo amor*, the fulfillment of *Homo sapiens*.

One Mountain is committed to articulating a Story of Value that can become the ground for the new society that must be birthed in response to the meta-crisis. We recognize that we are living at a pivotal moment in history. In this "time between stories," the great moral imperative is to tell the new Story of Value. It is ours to do, personally and collectively, with great trembling and ecstatic joy.

FROM DOGMA TO *DHARMA*: ETERNAL AND EVOLVING FIRST PRINCIPLES AND FIRST VALUES

The teachings are grounded in decades of deep study across many wisdom traditions. Over the years, week by week, these teachings were incrementally developed within the framework of the *One Mountain, Many Paths* broadcast. We often refer to these teachings as *Dharma*.

This word was originally used in lineage traditions to refer to something like universal law. This is a crucial realization: just as there is universal law in mathematical value, there is also a sense of universal law in ethics and value.

Historically, Dharma often devolved into unchanging dogma. Evolution was ignored, and the natural process of Dharma evolution became disconnected from its deep, eternal context. The weakness of the word Dharma is that too often it did not include the evolving insights of the sciences, it confused local cultural truths with universal truths, and it used words like "eternal," as in "eternal Tao," as opposed to words like "evolution."

Eternal came to mean unchanging, and that kind of thinking often led to overly ethnocentric readings of Dharma. Local systems would claim their religious and cultural insights as immutable, which stood in the way of the emergence of a genuine world Story of Value that is real, inherent to Cosmos, and backed by the Universe—even as it is also always evolving.

Or, as we often say, "eternal value is evolving value. The eternal Tao is the evolving Tao."

We have shown that, emergent from profound insights in the "interior sciences," eternal does not mean unchanging in time; it means what we call the deeper Field of ErosValue that is beneath culture, geography, and history, which lives beneath all individual and collective values, and beneath time and space itself.

As such, we have gradually transitioned from the term Dharma to the term *Value*, in the sense of the Field of Value that lives beneath all values. This Field of Value discloses as First Principles and First Values embedded in a Story of Value.

Indeed, as the interior sciences knew and the exterior sciences imply, Reality arises in a Field of ErosValue in which an entire set of mathematical, musical, molecular, moral, and mystical values are the very ground of all being. That Field of Value is eternal—the true ground of the Good, True and Beautiful—even as it is evolving.

But of course, it is equally critical not just to talk about evolving value, but to ground the evolving value in its true nature, the eternal Field of First Principles and First Values, always reaching for ever-more life, ever-more love, ever-more care, ever-more depth, ever-more uniqueness, ever-more intimate communion, and ever-more transformation.

As such, when we refer to the word Dharma, which still appears in these texts together with the word value, we refer to an evolving Dharma grounded in an *eternal and evolving* Field of Value. Indeed, eternity and evolution are two faces of the whole, opposites joined at the hip, that characterize the nature of our Cosmos in virtually all of its expressions.

It's in these terms that we ground a robust world philosophy that integrates the validated, leading-edge insights of premodern traditional wisdom, modern wisdom, and more recent postmodern insights, weaving them together into a new whole greater than the sum of its parts.

This new whole is a shared Story of Value rooted in First Principles and First Values that are both eternal and evolving.

These First Principles and First Values of Cosmos are woven together into a new Story of Value as a context for our diversity, a new Universe Story. This new Story gives us the best possible responses we have to the mystery, and to the great questions:

- Who am I? Who are we?
- Where am I? Where are we?
- What should I do? What should we do?

It is only through such a shared Universe Story—a narrative of identity and ethos as a context for our blessed diversity—that we can realize how what unites is so much greater than what divides us.

Only a new Story of Value will allow us to both respond to the meta-crisis and participate together in birthing the most true, good, and beautiful world that we already know is possible.

THIS ORAL ESSAYS SERIES IS AN ENTRYWAY TO THE GREAT LIBRARY OF COSMOEROTIC HUMANISM

This Oral Essays series is part of the overarching project of the Great Library at the Center for World Philosophy and Religion, led by Dr. Marc Gafni, together with Dr. Zak Stein. The aim of the Great Library project is to articulate a robust and comprehensive new Story of Value, CosmoErotic Humanism, in the form of dozens of well-researched and extensively footnoted academic works.

Our vision is to provide the philosophical framework that will be vital for navigating humanity through this time of immense crisis and transformation.

To begin your journey into CosmoErotic Humanism, we tenderly refer you to the book *First Principles and First Values*, co-authored by Marc Gafni, Zak Stein, and Ken Wilber, under the name David J. Temple. David J. Temple is a pseudonym created for enabling ongoing collaborative authorship at the Center for World Philosophy and Religion. The two primary authors behind David J. Temple are Marc Gafni and Zak Stein, and for different projects, specific writers will be named as part of the collaboration, such as Ken Wilber and others.

Three other volumes complete this introduction: *A Return to Eros*, by Marc Gafni and Kristina Kincaid; *Your Unique Self*, by Marc Gafni; and *Education in a Time between Worlds*, by Zak Stein.

We hope that the Oral Essays in this volume, with their informal style of transmission, will serve as an allurement and entryway for you into the more formal books of the Great Library that provide the robust intellectual underpinnings of the new Story of Value.

A NOTE ABOUT THE EDITORS

This Oral Essays collection has been edited by students of the new Story of CosmoErotic Humanism. Each of us has actively participated in *One Mountain, Many Paths*, and most of us have been in deep "Holy of Holies" study with Dr. Marc Gafni for many years.

We have been privileged to find ourselves well-versed in the teachings, and even emerging as lineage-holders of CosmoErotic Humanism.[3]

We view this editing project as a privilege and a deep practice of study and clarification. We experience ourselves as a *mystical editing society*, frequently meeting and conversing together about the content—the depth of knowledge and wisdom offered here—as well as the technical intricacies involved with publishing a beautiful and coherent series of books. In so doing, we function as a "Unique Self Symphony," which itself is a Dharmic

---

3 CosmoErotic Humanism is a world philosophical movement aimed at reconstructing the collapse of value at the core of global culture. Much like Romanticism or Existentialism, CosmoErotic Humanism is not merely a theory but a movement that changes the very mood of Reality. It is an invitation to participate in evolving the source code of consciousness and culture towards a cosmocentric *ethos* for a planetary civilization.

The term CosmoErotic Humanism, initially coined by Dr. Gafni and colleagues, points to a complex, multi-faceted, layered, and nuanced evolutionary set of insights that has evolved over decades of intensive research, teaching, and spiritual practice from deep within a wide range of wisdom traditions (including the Wisdom of Solomon lineage tradition, Bodhisattva Buddhism, and Kashmir Shaivism), as well as multiple disciplines including complexity theory, chaos theory, emergence theory, molecular biology, and the more classical disciplines of the humanities.

The seeds of CosmoErotic Humanism were planted with Dr. Marc Gafni's work on a two-volume, 1,000-page opus called *Radical Kabbalah* (Integral Publishers, 2012). This scholarly work, sourced from deep study within the esoteric lineage texts of the Wisdom of Solomon, points to a non-dual, or acosmic, realization which—unlike the prevailing conceptualization of non-duality—does not efface the human being; rather, it is highly humanistic in its nature. The next step in the evolution of CosmoErotic Humanism was the insight that all of Reality is evolving Eros, which lives in, as, and through the human being.

A failure of Eros leads inexorably to the creation of narratives of "pseudo-eros." CosmoErotic Humanism is a response to the modern mental and social breakdown sourced in the proliferation of multiple forms of pseudo-eros and its broken narratives, such as rivalrous conflict governed by win/lose metrics and the dogmatic denial of intrinsic value in Cosmos, which together generate our current "global intimacy disorder."

term that connotes an omni-considerate collaboration between realized Unique Selves synergizing our unique gifts into a new emergence greater than the sum of the parts. Even as we worked diligently to standardize our editing styles, meeting on a weekly basis to debate the nuances of phrasing, we also operated from within a deep appreciation of the unique style that each editor brought to his or her work. As such, the reader might notice some variation in editing style among the books.

Please note that Dr. Marc Gafni has not reviewed these edited Oral Essays, as he is deeply engaged in writing the formal books of the Great Library. But he has been generous in responding to questions and providing overall guidance in the project. Overall, as Marc's students and students of the Dharma, we have made it a key project at the Center to publish these pieces of work relatively independently.

OUR UNIQUE ORAL-ESSAY EDITING STYLE PRESERVES THE ENERGY OF THE ORIGINAL TRANSMISSION

Dr. Marc Gafni is a uniquely gifted teacher whose oral transmission is imbued with a quality that has proven transformative for his students. Many of us feel mystically transformed by both the content and the underlying energy of the transmission style. Therefore, as we like to say, *trust the magic ways the Dharma comes through your unique understanding!*

As Marc's empowered students, colleagues, and beloved friends, we have a deep knowing that these teachings are vital for the survival and thriving of humanity as we know it, and we recognize the importance of publishing his teachings in a written format that will be accessible by future generations. At the same time, we sought to preserve the Eros of the original oral transmission with all of its nuance, power, and depth. Our intention in the editing process, to the greatest extent possible, has been to keep these spoken artifacts intact in order to maintain the flow of the original transmission. We have therefore chosen not to engage in intensive formal editing, as we found that doing so resulted in the loss of the energetic transmission that is so key to fully receiving the Dharma.

After experimenting with many ways to present these texts, we developed a specific way of laying out the text on the page. Marc, in collaboration with Zak Stein and Russian intellectual/artist Elena Maslova-Levin—and ultimately all of the editors, through many conversations—developed a unique, artistic presentation of the text, using bolding, italics, bullet points, and other stylistic features which together serve to accentuate the immediacy of the oral transmission.

As part of this editing style, intended to preserve the integrity of the original transmission, we have refrained from removing the frequent recapitulations of key themes. We found that each recapitulation contributes something vital to the rhythm and music beneath the words, like the beating drum of our hearts. These recapitulations not only review previous material but also add important new emphases, perspectives, and elements of the new Story of Value. We ask for your patience as a reader to trust the rhythm of these texts, and we trust you as a reader to have the depth and steadiness to find your way through.

KEY COMPONENTS: LINK TO THE ORIGINAL BROADCAST, EVOLUTIONARY LOVE CODES AND PRAYER

To supplement the written word, each episode includes a QR code linking to the original broadcast on YouTube, as well as occasional links to featured songs and video clips.

Each episode also centers around an "Evolutionary Love Code," formulated by Marc. These codes are part of the ongoing articulation and distillation of the Dharma as it unfolds and emerges, week by week, over the course of many years, through the mystical process we call Outrageous Love or Evolutionary Love.

Another core component of the *One Mountain, Many Paths* episodes is what Marc and Barbara called "Evolutionary Prayer." Prayer is experienced in *One Mountain* not in the old fundamentalist sense of a "cosmic vending-machine god" who is alienated from Cosmos. Marc refers to this as the "god you do not and should not believe in"—and he often adds, "the god you don't believe in does not exist."

GOD IS THE INFINITE INTIMATE

In fact, in the Dharma of CosmoErotic Humanism, a new name for God has emerged: the "Infinite Intimate," who appears in first-, second-, and third-person expressions. Marc first shared this name as he heard it whispered in 2023, although earlier intimations and formulations of the name appeared as early as 2010.

In first person, God is infinitely alive and as intimate as our own first-person experience.

In second person, God is the infinitely intimate Personhood of Cosmos that knows our name and holds us—the God about whom we say, *whenever we fall, we fall into Her hands.* This is the God who is our Beloved, Father, Mother, Lover, and Evolutionary Partner.

Finally, in third person, God inheres in all of the First Principles and First Values of Cosmos, and in the laws of science (both interior and exterior) that govern manifest Reality.

Therefore, we have a realization of God as not only the Infinity of Power but also the Infinity of Intimacy.

In *One Mountain, Many Paths*, we are reclaiming prayer at a higher level of consciousness. And we are reclaiming prayer as deep, alive, loving, and intimate conversation7

s with God as the Infinite Intimate who knows our name.

REFLECTING ON THE CO-CREATION BETWEEN
DR. MARC GAFNI AND BARBARA MARX HUBBARD

Barbara and Marc met five years before Barbara passed. As Barbara said so often, "before I met Marc, I was sure that I was done." Barbara had taught so beautifully for decades, focusing particularly on a powerful articulation of "conscious evolution." Indeed, it would not be inaccurate to say that Barbara was the greatest storyteller of conscious evolution of her time.

Conscious evolution was also a premise in Marc's thinking, but drawn from an entirely different set of sources and experiences. Barbara drew from the classical sources of evolutionary spirituality, such as Teilhard de Chardin, Buckminster Fuller, and many others. Indeed, she was closely associated with Fuller, and was perhaps de Chardin's most ardent intellectual devotee.

Marc drew a somewhat different vision of conscious evolution from the interior sciences of the great wisdom traditions, with a primary emphasis on what he refers to as the "Solomon lineages," merged together with careful readings of the leading edges of the sciences. In the old version of conscious evolution, the movement from unconscious to conscious was a movement of evolution by chance to evolution by choice.

Together Marc and Barbara evolved the old version of conscious evolution, pointing out that evolution itself was always in some sense conscious, but as Marc formulated it, the awakening to conscious evolution refers to the awakening of evolution as human consciousness, coupled with the human realization of being conscious evolution in person, and the human capacity to locate oneself within the context of the larger evolutionary story.

Marc focused his attention on an entirely different dimension of Reality, which he and his colleagues began to call CosmoErotic Humanism. The Intimate Universe, Homo amor, Unique Self and Unique Self Symphonies, God as the Infinity of Intimacy, Eros and the CosmoErotic Universe, distinctions like Role Mate, Soul Mate and Whole Mate, the Four Selves,

Evolutionary Love, Outrageous Love, Evolution: the Love Story of the Universe, First Principles and First Values, Evolving Perennialism, the Evolution of Love, and many more are terms articulated by Gafni and shared with Barbara in their conversation, study, and creative engagement.

Some terms they coined together, for example "a Planetary Awakening in Love through Unique Self Symphonies," where Gafni described Unique Self Symphonies, and Barbara aligned her vision of a planetary Pentecost to Marc's vision of Unique Self Symphonies.

Other key terms were unique and articulated by Barbara, for example: conscious evolution, teleros, telerotic, from joining genes to joining genius, regenopause, vocational arousal, birthing of humanity, synergy engine, and of course her work around what she called the Wheel of Co-creation.

Ultimately, Marc and Barbara attempted to synergize their work in what they called the Wheel of Co-creation 2.0. Barbara and Marc experienced themselves as merging their respective Dharma into what they began to refer to as conscious evolution 2.0, or later, CosmoErotic Humanism.

The first 129 episodes of One Mountain, Many Paths took place in the last period of Barbara's life and reflect the depth and texture of the stunning evolutionary whole-mate meeting between her and Marc. As Barbara was deep in study with Marc, a lot of what she shared in Evolutionary Church was the Dharma of their deep study and collaboration. Although sometimes it may be clear who is speaking, we generally publish these early episodes in what we are calling "one voice."

The first 129 episodes, with Marc and Barbara together, have been grouped chronologically. Episodes 130 to 400 and onwards, which were transmitted by Marc, have been grouped by topic.

THE INVITATION

We invite you to find your way into this revolution. Each one of our Unique Selves and unique gifts are desperately needed as we co-create this new Story of Value together, as part of the covenant between generations, for the sake of the whole.

Let's *play a larger game* and evolve the very source code of consciousness and culture together.

With mad love,

The Editors

LOVE OR DIE

LOCATING OURSELVES: ARTICULATING THE ESSENTIAL CONTEXT FOR THE ONE MOUNTAIN, MANY PATHS ORAL ESSAYS

SETTING OUR INTENTION

Intention setting is everything.

We're here—as da Vinci was with his cohort in the Renaissance—**to play a larger game, to participate in the evolution of love, which is to tell the new Story of Value rooted in First Principles and First Values.**

- ◆ Our intention is to recognize the critical historical juncture in which we find ourselves.
- ◆ Our intention is to take our seat at the table of history and to say, *we take responsibility for this.*
- ◆ Our intention is to participate as revolutionaries for the sake of the whole.

What we're here to do is revolution; revolution for the sake of the evolution of love.

It's a revolution for the sake of the trillions of unborn lives that will not manifest:

- The unborn loves
- The unborn creativity
- The unborn goodness
- The unborn truth
- The unborn beauty

All of it looks to us.

Not because we're engaged in grandiosity. Not at all!

- We're trembling before She.
- We're trembling with joy at the privilege.
- We're trembling with joy at the responsibility.
- We're trembling with joy at the Possibility of Possibility.
- We have to enact a new Story in this moment of time. Because it is only a new Story that can change the vector of history.

The most revolutionary act that we can do—the greatest moral imperative of this time—**is to articulate a new Story at this time between worlds and this time between stories.**

Story is not made up, as postmodernity suggests. **We all live in inescapable frameworks; our framework is the story we live in.** Right now, Reality lives according to win/lose metrics, a story that is generating existential risk. **We need to change that story.**

When we change that story, when we tell a new Story—not a made-up story, but a new Story of Value, rooted in First Principles and First Values—**then it all changes.**

We need to participate in the evolution of the source code of consciousness and culture, which is the evolution of love.

It's the most important, exciting, evolutionary, revolutionary act that we can do to alleviate suffering: to be lovers.

Like Rumi, the great poet of Sufism, we have to be "mad lovers," because it's the only sanity.

To be mad lovers is to see around the corner, to not be so obsessed with the details of the contractions of my life.

Let me see bigger.

Let me take complete care of myself in every possible way, let me completely attend to those in my circle of intimacy and influence, and then—*let me expand my circle.*

That's what we're here for.

- Our intention is to participate in the *LoveForce*, the *LoveIntelligence*, the *LoveBeauty*, the *LoveDesire* that literally animates Cosmos all the way up and all the way down.
- Our intention is to participate in the evolution of love.

> [*In the next few pages we will cover some key concepts which are essential to locating ourselves and setting the context for all the One Mountain, Many Paths Oral Essays. —Eds.*]

OVERVIEW: EROS IS NO LONGER A LUXURY—IT'S LOVE OR DIE

Eros is life.

The failure of Eros destroys life.

Our lack of Eros is poised to destroy the world.

All civilizations have fallen because the stories that they lived in were, in some sense, stories based on rivalrous conflict governed by win/lose metrics. Every civilization was weakened by interior polarization caused by the lack of a shared Story of Value.

We now have a global civilization, but we haven't created a shared Story of Value.

We haven't solved the generator functions that caused all civilizations to fall. Our global civilization has exponential technologies and extraction models depleting the Earth of resources that took billions of years to create, which is going to lead to a civilizational collapse.

Existential risk is risk to our very existence.

The choice is clear: love or die.

It's that simple.

Eros is no longer a luxury. It is an absolute necessity for the survival of the individual and the planet.

In the last half a century, modern psychology has documented an age-old truth: a fully nourished baby who is not held in loving arms will die.

So too, our world, both personal and global—even with all the resources of intelligence and technology at our disposal—will die without being held in love, in the embrace of Eros.

We must embrace a personal path of love and a global politics of love.

Not ordinary love. Not love which is "mere human sentiment," but Eros, or what we sometimes call Outrageous Love, which is the heart of existence itself.

We live in a world of outrageous pain.

The only response is Outrageous Love.

WHAT IS EROS?

Eros is the experience of radical aliveness, moving towards, seeking, desiring ever-deeper contact and ever-greater wholeness.[4] Eros is the core fabric of Reality's being and the motivational architecture of Reality's becoming.

Eros is what animates the evolutionary impulse itself, from the very inception of Cosmos all the way to our very selves, who awaken to the realization that the evolutionary impulse throbs uniquely in each of us.

The realization of human awakening and transformation that lies at the core of the interior sciences is the invitation—or even the urgent and desperate demand—of a madly loving Cosmos animated by infinities of power and infinities of intimacy.

The demand—the desperate invitation, the plea, the tender and fierce command of Cosmos that lives inside every human being—is to awaken: to awaken to our true nature as unique incarnations of Eros and Ethos that are needed and desperately desired by All-That-Is. Said slightly differently: Reality is Eros. Or: God is Eros.

The failure of Eros destroys life. The collapse of Eros is always the hidden (or not so hidden) root cause for the collapse of ethics.

This is true both personally and collectively. We live in a moment of a world-wide and personal collapse of Eros. Our lack of Eros is poised to destroy

---

4 We define Eros through what we refer to as the Eros equation (one of a series of what we call interior science equations):

> *Eros = Radical Aliveness* x *Desiring (Growing + Seeking)* x *Deeper Contact* x *Greater Wholeness* x *Self Actualization/Self Transcendence (Creation [Destruction])*

There are good reasons for the formal language of the interior science equations in these writings, and the reader is invited to explore them on their own, in particular, in our work, David J. Temple, *First Principles and First Values: Forty-Two Propositions on CosmoErotic Humanism, the Meta-Crisis, and the World to Come* (World Philosophy and Religion, 2024).

the world. Humanity is currently experiencing what has come to be known as existential risk, a risk to our very existence, or what I will refer to as the Second Shock of Existence.

EXISTENTIAL RISK: THE SECOND SHOCK OF EXISTENCE

The first shock of existence is the death of the human being—the realization that we will die, which dawns in human consciousness at the beginning of history. We are not talking about the biological fact of death but the *existential* realization of death. Although the interior sciences disclose that death is a portal between two days (there is vast empirical,[5] philosophical,[6] and anthro-ontological evidence[7] for the continuity of consciousness[8]), death is also, in our own direct surface experience, a stark end. And that is obviously not a bug but a feature in the system.

---

5   We refer to evidence gathered by the most serious of researchers, beginning with Henry and Edith Sedgwick at Cambridge University and William James at Harvard University, and continuing in highly rigorous form for the last 150 years, as recapitulated by Whiteheadian scholar David Ray Griffin in multiple volumes. See also, for example, Dean Radin, *Real Magic: Unlocking Your Natural Psychic Abilities to Create Everyday Miracles* (Potter/TenSpeed/Harmony, 2018), *The Conscious Universe: The Scientific Truth of Psychic Phenomena* (HarperCollins, 2010), and other books. Or see the earlier classic by Frederic William Henry Myers, *Human Personality and Its Survival of Bodily Death* (Longmans, Green, 1907).

6   This requires a cogent analysis of materialism and dualism, and the introduction of the far more cogent third possibility, which we have called "pan-interiority."

7   We discuss Anthro-Ontology in some depth in *First Principles and First Values*, and see also the fuller conversation in David J. Temple, *First Principles and First Values: Towards an Evolving Perennialism: Introducing the Anthro-Ontological Method*—both published by World Philosophy and Religion Press, in conjunction with Integral Publishers. For now, we will simply define it as an "innate and clear interior gnosis directly available to the human being."

8   See Dr. Marc Gafni and Dr. Zachary Stein's essay in preparation, "Beyond Death: Anthro-Ontology, Philosophy, and Empiricism." This essay is slated to appear in the book *Towards a World Religion: Homo Amor Essays.* The essay is also the ground for a larger book by the same authors, *Twelve Portals to Life Beyond Death: Responding to the Second Shock of Existence,* in which we discuss three forms of material: the empirical, the philosophical, and the anthro-ontological, and show how each form discredits the notion of death as the end.

Our first-person experience is that death ends this life. It is not the *totality* of our experience if we go deeper inside, but it is obviously intended to be the central, potent, and painful dimension of every human life. Indeed, as Ernest Becker potently reminded us, the denial of death is at our peril.

All the stories and all the plotlines and all the threads of living end at that moment. Whatever happens beyond, we have an actual experience of ending. **Paradoxically, that ending, the experience of the finality of mortality, is what presses us into life.** From the implicit demand of the first shock of existence, human beings were activated and pressed into creative emergence, and what emerged was all of human culture, both interior and exterior.

The second shock of existence is the realization of the potential death of all humanity. After all the stages of human history—matter, life, and mind in all of their stages of evolutionary unfolding—we have come to this place in the evolution of humanity, in which the gap between our exponentially expanding exterior technologies and our stalled (or even regressing) interior technologies of value has created dire catastrophic and existential risks.

This gap generates extraction models and exponential growth curves, rivalrous conflicts based on win/lose metrics, tragedies of the commons, and multipolar traps, in which everyone has to keep producing to the nth degree, including weaponized exponential threats to our very existence because we are afraid that the other parties are going to do it and not be transparent—hide it from us and then dominate us.

GENERATOR FUNCTIONS FOR EXISTENTIAL RISK

Let's outline clearly the main *generator functions for existential risk.*

Rivalrous conflicts governed by zero-sum, win/lose metrics. Rivalrous conflicts generate extraction models at the core of the economic system and exponential growth curves. Both of these drive and are driven by a contrived system of artificially manufactured desires and needs, delivered into culture by ever more precise forms of micro-targeting to individuals and groups through the ever more immersive environment of the internet.

Next, rivalrous conflicts and exponential growth curves animated by win/lose metrics generate **complicated, fragile world systems** highly vulnerable to myriad forms of collapse. Fragile local systems are made exponentially more fragile on a global level by our inability to meet global challenges with social, legal, political, economic, and ethical infrastructures that remain largely local.

All of this is a direct result of the failure to develop more adequate interior technologies that would be sufficiently compelling to displace "rivalrous conflict governed by win/lose metrics" as the motivational architecture for the human life world.

This failure has led to the conditions that will cause the implosion of systems that are already and quite literally on the brink of collapsing themselves. That's what we mean by the *second shock of existence*.

To recapitulate: the second shock of existence is not the death of the human being, but the potential death of humanity.

It is the *Death Star* moment of our species.

THE DECONSTRUCTION OF INTRINSIC VALUE

We stand in this moment poised between utopia and dystopia, at a time between worlds and a time between stories. We need a new Story of Value, eternal yet evolving, rooted in First Principles and First Values, which would become a universal grammar of value and a context for our diversity.

This is exactly what the Renaissance was. It was a time between worlds and a time between stories. In the Renaissance, we had recently been challenged by the Black Death, a pandemic that swept across Europe. The Black Death destroyed between a third to half of Europe and a huge part of

Asia. People died horrifically, brutally, in the streets. They had no idea how to meet this challenge, and so, in response to the Black Death, da Vinci and Ficino and their cohorts understood that they had to tell a new Story of Value.

That story was the story of modernity. Did they get it right?

+ They got part of it right, which birthed, to use Jürgen Habermas' phrase, "the dignities of modernity," such as new ways of gathering information and universal human rights.
+ But they also deconstructed the source of Value. They lost the basis for the Good, the True, and the Beautiful.

The basis used to be divine revelation: *God told us.* But this claim was owned by religion, and every religion began to overreach and over-claim. The revelation was thus often mediated through cultural categories and wasn't fully accurate.

Modernity threw out revelation, but was unable to establish a new basis for value.

Value was just assumed to be real. As it says in the founding document of the American Revolution: *We hold these truths to be self-evident*—that is, *we don't really have a basis for value; we just take it as a given.*

In other words, modernity took out a loan of social capital from the traditional world. The source of value was never worked out.

And then, gradually, value began to collapse.

+ The Universe Story began to collapse.
+ The belief that the Good, the True, and the Beautiful are real began to collapse.
+ The belief that Love is real began to collapse.

As Bertrand Russell is reported to have said, "I cannot see how to refute the arguments for the subjectivity of ethical values, but I find myself incapable of believing that all that is wrong with wanton cruelty is that I do not like it."

What do you do if you grew up in a world in which value is not real? A world without a source of value, without a Universe Story, without a story of human identity, without a story of desire, without a narrative of power?

In the words of W.B. Yeats, *the center does not hold*.

- You have a collapse at the very center of society, because you no longer have Eros.
- You no longer have a Reality in which value is real, and so you have this lingering sense of emptiness.
- You have a complete collapse at the very center.
- We become *the hollow men and the stuffed men*, gesture without form.

And that's the source of our current existential risk.

THE DEEPER ROOT CAUSE OF THE META-CRISIS: A GLOBAL INTIMACY DISORDER

Above, I have outlined the major generator functions of existential risk. But there is a deeper cause for the existential risk that lurks underneath the rivalrous conflict governed by win/lose metrics and the fragile systems they engender.

And we cannot take the Death Star down without discerning and addressing this. We have already alluded to this root cause above, but at this point we need to make it more explicit so that, from this context, the adequate root response will become clear.

Modernity threw out the revelation, but was unable to establish a new basis for value.

This ostensibly surprising statement can be understood in a few simple steps:

1. All of the catastrophic and existential risk challenges we face are global: from climate change to artificial intelligence, pandemics, systems collapse, and exponential arms races.
2. Every global challenge self-evidently requires a global solution.
3. Global solutions can only be implemented with global co-ordination.
4. Global co-ordination is impossible without global coherence.
5. Global coherence is only possible if there is a global resonance between the parts.
6. Global resonance is only possible if we have global intimacy.

ONLY A SHARED STORY OF VALUE CAN GENERATE GLOBAL INTIMACY

Global intimacy—just like intimacy in a couple—is only possible when there is a shared story.

Not just a shared history, but a shared Story of Value.

- It is only a shared global story that can generate a new emergent quality of intimacy: global intimacy.
- A shared Story of Value must be rooted in shared ordinating values, or what we have called evolving First Values and First Principles.
- Intimacy requires a shared grammar of value as a matrix for a shared Story of Value.

The global intimacy disorder is the root cause for existential risk. The global intimacy disorder underlies the core generator functions for existential risk.

The global intimacy disorder is rooted in the failure to experience ourselves in a field of shared intrinsic value. This failure derives from the deconstruction of value.

Indeed, it is wholly accurate to say that **the root cause of the two generator functions of existential risk is the failed story of intrinsic value, or what we might also call the breakdown of Eros.**

1. The first generator function is **the success story**. Our modern success story is rivalrous conflict governed by win/lose metrics, which violates all the terms of the Intimacy Equation: there is no shared identity and no mutuality of recognition, feeling, value or purpose, and instead of *relative* otherness, there is *alienated* otherness. Such a story generates complicated fragile systems with no allurement or intimacy between the parts, systems which optimize for efficiency (as an expression of win/lose metrics) and not for resiliency and life.

2. The second generator function is **the deconstruction of intrinsic value** itself. The deconstruction of value is the sense that human value does not participate in the intrinsic value of the Real, for the Real is dogmatically declared to have no intrinsic value. Thus, there is no shared identity between the interior of the human being and Reality. There is no common participation in a field of shared intrinsic value. Instead of being intimate with value, we are alienated from value. And only intrinsic value can arouse will: political, moral, and social will.

To sum up, without a shared grammar of value there is no global intimacy, and therefore no global coherence, and no global coordination in response to catastrophic and existential risk, which means, put simply, there will be, quite literally, no future.

HEALING THE GLOBAL INTIMACY DISORDER
REQUIRES THE EVOLUTION OF INTIMACY

But we are not hopeless. On the contrary, we are filled with great hope. Hope is a memory of the future. That memory of the future *is* the direct hit that takes down the Death Star, the culture of death. **The direct hit must be**—as it has always been in history—**the emergence of a new stage of evolution**.

Crisis is an evolutionary driver, and every crisis is, at its core, a crisis of intimacy: from the oxygen crisis of the single cells dying which generated multicellular life at the dawn of existence, to the existential risk in this very moment.[9]

The direct hit is therefore structurally self-evident: the evolution of intimacy itself.

What is intimacy, as a structure of Cosmos all the way down and all the way up the evolutionary chain? We engage this inquiry in depth in other writings, but for now we will simply adduce what we have called the "Intimacy Equation":

> *Intimacy = shared identity in the context of [relative] otherness x mutuality of recognition x mutuality of pathos x mutuality of value x mutuality of purpose*

Intimacy is about the capacity of parts to generate a *shared identity* while retaining their otherness, or distinct identity. This requires multiple mutualities, including recognition, pathos (or feeling), value, and purpose. The parts must recognize and feel each other, even as they share value and purpose. But all of this must lead to intimate union—and not pathological

---

9 We demonstrate this principle in some depth in the multi-volume series, *The Universe: A Love Story* (forthcoming) (https://worldphilosophyandreligion.org/early-ontologies), *The Intimate Universe: Global Intimacy Disorder as Cause for Global Action Paralysis* (forthcoming), and in other writings of CosmoErotic Humanism.

fusion, where the distinct identity of the parts disappears—like subatomic particles that successfully become an atom, or two people who successfully become a couple.

THE DECONSTRUCTION OF VALUE IS THE DECONSTRUCTION OF INTIMACY

We have identified the global intimacy disorder as the root cause of existential risk. But the underlying ultimate failure of intimacy is the deconstruction of value itself.

The deconstruction of value means that human value does not participate in any sense of intrinsic value of the Real. This is not about individual *values,* but about *the Field of Value* that underlies all of them. **When the human being**—moved, often sincerely or even nobly, by myriad cultural, historical, and psychological confusions—**claims to have stepped out of the Field of Value, then intimacy itself is deconstructed.**

The deconstruction of value is the deconstruction of intimacy.

In the absence of a shared Story of Value, a story that is an authentic expression of Reality's Eros, a story rooted in *pseudo-Eros* takes center stage and becomes the generator function for existential risk. Our modern pseudo-Eros story is *rivalrous conflict governed by win/lose metrics.* Such a story catalyzes in its wake the second generator function of existential risk: *complicated fragile systems with no allurement or intimacy between the parts.* It is in that sense that we have argued that the first generator function for existential risk is the success story.

- The failure of intimacy is precisely the impotent experience that there is no shared identity between the interior of the human being and Reality. **There is no shared identity in the sense of any kind of common participation in a field of shared intrinsic value.**
- **But only a shared Story of Value can arouse the global will**

required to engage catastrophic and existential risk. For it is only global political, moral, and social will—and we can even say *erotic* will—that can generate the most Good, True and Beautiful world that we have always known is possible.

THE EVOLUTION OF LOVE IS THE TELLING OF A NEW STORY

Coupled with the Intimacy Equation is the scientifically grounded realization, in both the exterior and interior sciences, that Reality is a progressive deepening of intimacies, or, said slightly differently:

Reality is Evolution. Evolution is the evolution of intimacy.

- The evolution of intimacy requires—both personally and collectively—a deeper, more accurate discernment of the nature of our universe, ourselves, and our beloveds.
- This new discernment generates a new global Story of Value.
- The new global Story of Value generates an emergent, heretofore unseen global intimacy and heals the global intimacy disorder.

The new Story of Value is the direct hit that takes down the Death Star and replaces it with the hope that invokes the memory of our best future.

Global intimacy facilitates global coherence, which facilitates global coordination, which activates the possibility of our creative and effectively coordinated global responses to the global meta-crisis in its entirety and its specific expressions.

To solve Bertrand Russell's challenge—the apparent argument for the subjectivity of ethical values—**we have to reground value theory in eternal yet evolving First Principles and First Values, and articulate a new Story of Value**.

This is what we call CosmoErotic Humanism.

CosmoErotic Humanism—together with other emergent strands—**needs to become the ground of a world religion as a context for our diversity**. We need religion, even as we need science, to articulate a shared global grammar of value.

As we said at the beginning, our choice is simple: love or die.

- To love means to participate in the evolution of love, which is the evolution of the human Story of Value.
- To love means to evolve and activate a new cultural enlightenment—rooted in a new narrative of identity, a new narrative of value, a new narrative of intimate communion, a new narrative of desire, a new narrative of power—all of which will birth new narratives of economics and politics.
- The evolution of love is the telling of a new Story.

The new Story that must be told is a love story, for in fact that is the deepest truth of Reality, rooted in the best exterior and interior sciences, that we have at this moment in time:

- Reality is not merely a fact. Reality is a story.
- Reality is not an ordinary story. Reality is a love story.
- Reality is not an ordinary love story. Reality is an Outrageous Love Story.

Story doesn't mean it's *made-up*.

It means doing the hard work of integrating the validated insights of the traditional world, the modern world, and the postmodern world.

This is the intention at the heart of telling the new Story of CosmoErotic Humanism.

ABOUT THIS VOLUME

This volume of edited "oral essays"—lightly edited transcripts based on *One Mountain, Many Paths* transmissions—begins with a memorial service to Barbara Marx Hubbard. In this volume, we honor her passing and her deep contributions to *conscious evolution*, focusing on the personal gnosis and realization that "I am evolution in person." We points particularly to Barbara's distinction between joining genes and joining genius, and to her notion of *generating social synergy by bringing together what is already working* (the leading-edge innovations in every field) as a core mechanism of conscious evolution.

This volume focuses, however, on CosmoErotic Humanism's[1] next stage in the articulation of conscious evolution, what we often call Conscious Evolution 2.0. This is the realization of what he calls Evolution: The Love Story of the Universe. In CosmoErotic Humanism, we articulate the realization of conscious evolution as a love story—not an ordinary love story but an Outrageous Love story. Outrageous Love is the realization that our love is not mere human sentiment, but the heart of existence itself.

The stories of love that reduced Eros to mere human sentiment do not have the power to hold us at this time between worlds and time between stories, in this moment of meta-crisis (a series of interlocking social, political, educational and technological crises) that threatens both the death of humanity and the death of our humanity.

---

1   David J. Temple, *First Principles and First Values: Forty-Two Propositions on CosmoErotic Humanism* (2024).

Indeed, fundamental to the new story is the intuitive gnosis that evolution is nothing other than the evolution of love. This is the new love story.

In this book (where Barbara is featured posthumously in this book through a series of recordings) we propose that "Reality moves towards resurrection" through an ongoing process of evolutionary development. This is the "good news" that Barbara offered, precisely at humanity's eleventh hour, a time when humanity is "poised at the abyss" and is thus called upon to evolve consciously. Barbara was perhaps the greatest storyteller of conscious evolution in the twentieth century. In Barbara's understanding, conscious evolution was evolution waking up to consciousness through us. Humanity is called to directly, humbly and audaciously take the reins of the future.

Central to this vision is the birth of the new human, what CosmoErotic Humanism refers to as *Homo amor*, the new human and new humanity. Originally we deployed the term *Homo amor universalis*—the next necessary stage of humanity's evolution. This birthing of the new human represents what CosmoErotic Humanism refers as the fourth Big Bang. This is the very core of our collective response to what we are calling the "second shock of existence." The first shock of existence is the realization of our biological death. The second shock of existence is potential death of humanity. Or, in an alternative scenario of second shock, it's the death of *our* humanity, the snuffing out of what makes us human.

Homo amor is balanced between breakthrough and breakdown. *Homo amor* feels the outrageous pain of the world. And *Homo amor* embodies the Outrageous Love which is the only response to outrageous pain—hence the dharmic phrase which lies the very core of CosmoErotic Humanism: **We live in a world of outrageous pain; the only response is Outrageous Love.**

Homo amor is empirically sensual, capacitated for sensemaking, devoted to drawing clear distinctions, reuniting Eros and gnosis, and joining genius to embody the shift to the next stage of human evolution and the evolution of love.

Central to the diagnosis of our current moment is the "global intimacy disorder," where we've forgotten "what it means to touch each other." We have lost access to the truth that we are always ever already touching each other—heart, mind, body and soul. This is a time of rampant addiction, myriad forms of "pseudo-eros." Pseudo-erotic forms of connection that do not partake of the fundamental Field of Value at the heart of Reality are the fabric of our everyday lives. We've also forgotten that *we are literally all in this together.*

Of course, for *Homo amor* merely opening our hearts, while necessary, is not sufficient to respond to this moment. No one and no part of ourselves can be excluded. Re-establishing an erotic wholeness, where no one and nothing is outside of the circle, is the main task for *Homo amor* at the leading edge of conscious evolution.

Homo amor is willing to step in and play a larger game, and the game is none other than participating in the evolution of love or Reality itself.

How do we know what to do? It becomes clearer when we realize that we are responding to a singular question: "What does evolution need from me in this next moment?" All answers are in response to this one question. Reality always needs my unique gifts at any given moment. I can, however, only give my unique gift if I'm willing to take my unique risk and clarify my deepest heart's desire. But when that happens, a new intimate communion begins to arise. Unique Selves[2] begin to come together as Unique Self Symphonies, wholes infinitely greater than the mere sum of their parts.

Through the articulation of the Evolutionary Love Codes in this book, the invitations to prayer in new forms and through practical exercises, you will come to recognize that love is not merely an emotion but a perception. You will develop the capacity to *see with God's eyes*, to see the next steps in the evolution of love, to see the new synergies that will allow a deepening of intimacy—ultimately leading to a "Planetary Awakening in Love."

---

2 Marc Gafni, *Your Unique Self: the Radical Path to Personal Enlightenment* (2012).

Finally, we can view God from first-, second- and third-person perspectives: God who lives in me in first person, God who is *the space in between* myself and all of my beloveds, and God who is the erotic force animating the self-actualizing Cosmos in every second of the evolutionary journey. God is Good, True, and Beautiful. God is the Infinity of Power calling us to our greatness. But God is no less *the Infinity of Intimacy* into whose arms we are always falling and to whom we are always on our knees.

Volume 14

These oral essays are edited talks delivered by Marc Gafni and Barbara Marx Hubbard between April and June 2019.

CHAPTER ONE

BARBARA'S MEMORIAL IN EVOLUTIONARY CHURCH

Episode 131 — April 13, 2019

BELOVED BARBARA

Welcome everyone! Every week, we've been doing Evolutionary Church. It's been—for Barbara, myself, and thousands of us, about 10,000 of us from around the world—the heart and the throb of where we're going and the vision we want to articulate together.

Barbara and I loved Evolutionary Church. Every week, we would write a code together. We're now in Evolutionary Church, so for those of you who are wondering what to expect, there are going to be two memorial services.

This week, I spent the entire week in a very painful and difficult process. Barbara passed on Wednesday. It was very sudden. Barbara had said to me, **"When I pass, have a memorial service at church and have a big evolutionary party."**

We're going to do a second kind of *evolutionary party*. At that evolutionary party, we're going to see lots of Barbara's work and clips.

Now we're in church, and we're going to follow the order of church.

Imagine you are at my good friend Michael Beckwith's church, *Agape*, and Michael is doing the memorial service. You follow the order of church.

For those of you, the few hundred people who are with us every week, you know the order. But there are at least an extra two or three hundred people who are all here for Barbara. **After all, everyone has really shown up for Barbara. I really want to just feel Barbara's delight. There's no question that Barbara has shown up here and that Barbara, you're with us.** This is the first memorial service that we said we would do in church that you loved so much.

So, our order of service:

- There's a *dharma* recap, then Barbara would resonate the code that we wrote together, usually the night before—that's the resonance.
- Then we move into prayer.
- We established the principles of this Evolutionary Church, this evolutionary communion.
- Then we do a hymn with Leonard Cohen, who works with us in the church, the holy and the broken *Hallelujah*!
- And we pray.
- Then we would usually do two sermons on a shared resonant theme, which was about articulating the Evolutionary Love Codes that are the core of the new story of humanity.

Today, in place of the sermons, I'll gently, humbly offer a eulogy to Barbara, and all throughout, we're going to be resonating with Barbara, who is here with us.

Now what's happening is, just to find and introduce the code, Barbara has been silenced for a moment by death.

Anyone who knew Barbara knew that what she believed in most passionately, what she lived, and what she always told me:

> *Marc, I'm not going down to be there in a grave with worms, and I'm not going up to sit with angels in heaven. I am the continuity of consciousness. I declare the continuity of consciousness!*

"And I declare!" Barbara would say. *Do you all remember that word? "I declare!"* Just a few days ago, we heard Barbara speaking about it. So, Barbara, right at this moment, we declare with you the continuity of your consciousness and know that you're here with us.

Last Friday night I was talking to Barbara about the code for the next day. The next morning, I called, and Barbara wasn't vocal, and they didn't quite understand why. I asked the nurse to put her on the phone. They held the phone to her ear, and Barbara said, *Marc!* She was excited about church, and then she wasn't able to speak afterwards.

Ultimately, she went into a coma, wasn't able to wake up, and began her transition. But Barbara is not silent. **Her silence in this moment is not a silence of absence; it's a silence of presence. It's up to *us* to carry that torch.** *Each of us* **has shared work together.**

But today, for all of the people who've known Barbara for their whole lives, Barbara is passing the torch. And every single person in this church today is invited to what Barbara called, *their vocational arousal* in order for each of us to light the world on fire with that teaching, with that message, with that aliveness, with that Barbara-ness.

Barbara now shifts, not to silence of absence, but to silence of presence. **Barbara is going to become more present in her continuity of consciousness, more available, more alive, and more impactful than even ever before.**

I'm just going to invite everyone to the chat box just to feel Barbara here, friends. I'm going to ask everyone just to write three words. Not in the past tense, not "inspired me." Not in the past, Barbara is present.

So, how about everyone writing into the chat box, *Barbara inspires me!*

We can feel Barbara here. *Barbara inspires me!* **Let's just feel that.**

It's not silence of absence. We're actually triumphing over death. The triumph over death was one of Barbara's deepest heart's desires. We'll talk about heart's desire.

Barbara inspires me! Feel that! Feel that just ripple. Let's lift that like a prayer to the sky: *Barbara inspires me! Barbara inspires me!* Just let it rip! Let it rip beautifully.

For people who haven't been in Evolutionary Church before, let me share something about Barbara, about church, so you'll understand.

I couldn't capture Barbara's essence as the great evolutionary thinker of our time. It's actually not quite accurate. Barbara's role that we talked about many times, wasn't to be an original evolutionary thinker. That's not how she viewed herself.

I believe **Barbara was the greatest *Evolutionary Storyteller* of our time.** Barbara was the feminine co-creator. She thought beautifully. She had a clear, sharp, and wonderful mind.

Anyone who's read *Evolutionary Synthesis,*[1] which she wrote in 2007 and is about 45 pages, you'll see the beauty and clarity as she gathered thoughts, extensively cited, and wove the thoughts together.

Barbara's essence was Barbara inspired.

---

1 You can access it here: https://greattransitionstories.org/wp-content/uploads/sites/13/2018/06/Evolutionary_Synthesis_BMH_2.21.pdf.

Barbara told the Evolutionary Story. Barbara became the campfire.[2] Barbara became the Word. She was the *Logos*.

Barbara inspires me!

Mysticism and all great traditions teach that the challenge of death lies in a person becoming static, no longer able to influence or impact the world. Therefore, in mysticism, our practice is to offer strength and energy to the departed—in this instance, to the great leader, visionary, and wondrous woman who has passed, our beloved Barbara—to aid her in taking the next step on the journey of the continuity of consciousness.

She's turning to us now and saying, *Activate me!* She's saying, *Let me impact you so that I'm fully alive.* So, when we write *Barbara inspires me!* It directly impacts and affects all the worlds, upper and lower. It supercharges. It animates Barbara's consciousness to take the next steps.

Barbara inspires me! We're ready to be impacted. We're going to follow the pattern of church today.

We're going to have a second much more formal memorial where we're going to play many of Barbara's clips and do the memorial in that sense.

But now we're in church, the church that we founded together.

We're going to follow the order of church.

- So, in this moment we are going to read the resonant code.
- We're going to go to prayer.
- I'll speak about the mandate of the church, very briefly.
- We'll talk briefly about prayer as we do every week, and we'll move into the prayer itself.
- Then we'll move into the eulogy itself: *Barbara inspires me!*

---

2   This is metaphoric language and is a poetic way of saying they became a central, transformative, unifying presence—offering warmth, wisdom, or connection to those around them, taking on the role of storytelling or wisdom-keeping.

BEFORE PRAYER

To love God is to know God. To love and to know—it's the same; it's One.

We're going to talk about the code in the context of Barbara's eulogy.

Our three words for this entire service: *Barbara inspires me!*

In Evolutionary Church, we turn to prayer, and we turn to Evolutionary Church. **It's a church, a synagogue, a mosque, a secular humanist center, and an activist center.**

Evolutionary Church is the place where we know that which unites us is so much greater than that which divides us.

Let it be clear to everyone—this is an Evangelical church.

It's Evangelical. If you knew Barbara, Barbara was an evolutionary evangelist. Apple Computer had Apple evangelists, we have fundamentalist evangelists. Barbara was an Evolutionary Evangelical.

The evangelist is bringing the Good News, but not in a regressive way. Barbara was about the Good News, and Barbara herself *was* the Good News; she was the *Word*. She was radical positivity. She was *Yes!* She was that unrelenting radical positivity that spoke the Good News, the utter goodness of Reality. Barbara was the Big Bang, the great flaring forth and banging! And the word at the center was *Yes!*

When the world moved from the unmanifest to the manifest—the world, Reality, Divinity—was saying *Yes!*

Here in Evolutionary Church and in the new *dharma* that we're unfolding together as we join a genius, we speak of God. We say *the god you don't believe in doesn't exist.* **We speak of God not as the Infinity of Power but God as the Infinity of Intimacy.**

6

In the Renaissance, da Vinci and his cohorts couldn't go to every village in Europe to heal the Black Plague, which decimated and caused unimaginable suffering. But they knew that to respond to suffering—to respond to outrageous pain—you need Outrageous Love.

We understand that Outrageous Love is to tell a new story; the Outrageous Lover tells a new story. Da Vinci and his cohorts told the story of modernity, the story that took us to the next step. It was a momentous leap.

Here, every week as we stand between dystopia and utopia, evolution seeks to evolve.

We tell the story of the evolution of intimacy. We tell the story of God. It's not a story in a fanciful sense. It's not conjecture. It's *dharma*—not dogma—in the sense of the best integration of all the deepest insights of the premodern, modern, and postmodern world, integrated into a larger whole, greater than the sum of the parts. This is what intimacy means.

Intimacy means *parts come together in a new shared identity,* which creates a whole that is greater than the sum of the parts. There's joy in telling the new story. **It's taking the parts from every period of history, the deepest, validated truths, weaving them together in the new story.** That's the Good News.

If the Good News is that postmodernity, with all of its great insights—which claims that we are post-truth and that everything is a social construction of Reality—actually was true *in part,* because *code* deconstructed the false power narratives.

But "No! No! No!" said Barbara. No!" says the Evolutionary Church. "No!" say so many of us gathered who are in their way telling the new story.

There is actually a new story. There's a new story, and that new story is an evangelical story, not in a regressive sense, in a progressive sense. It's the Good News. It's the shared truths.

In that new story, God is at the center, God who lives in us, as us, and through us, God who is already 'That'.

In that very beautiful sense, Barbara incarnated God/Goddess. Barbara was always *already there—tat tvam asi*, "Thou Art That." Barbara was already *That*. Barbara was completely and all too human, like all of us are. **We are all imperfect vessels for the light, but Barbara was at the same time, living and incarnating that *Yes!* That resounding *Yes!***

God lives in us in the first-person; God is the third person of the evolutionary impulse (what Julian Huxley called the evolutionary impulse and Barbara greatly championed the last 50 years).

> God is the evolutionary impulse, God in third person, the pulsing force of the creative Cosmos that unfolds to ever new and higher levels of emergence, that moves from simplicity to complexity, into higher and higher levels of freedom, consciousness, and order...

This is the way Barbara loved to say it. When she said it, she said, "I have absolute faith."

She spoke as an Evolutionary Evangelical. Absolute faith, that! That which took us from subatomic particles to Shakespeare is not going to stop creating now. **That creation becomes conscious through us.**

Barbara championed—more than any other single human being—conscious evolution. Not that evolution was never conscious. **Evolution was always conscious.** But evolution becomes conscious *through us*.

We become aware that the creative impulse lives in us, that evolution awakens in us, in person; that's the first and third-person of the Divine.

But here in Evolutionary Church, we're going the next step. We're realizing what Rumi knew and what Barbara knew when she was in the monastery and she wrote in her book, *Emergence: The Shift from Ego to Essence,* which captures it beautifully: *Every day is devoted to the Beloved.*

God is not only the Infinity of Power. God is not only the evolutionary impulse. God not only is the *That,* the *That-ness,* the *Such-ness,* that lives in us, as us, and through us. Rumi and Barbara, every morning, would want to fall into the arms of the Beloved.

She wrote, "Dear Beloved," and Rumi and Hafiz would fall into the arms of the Beloved. The Beloved is not *That* of *tat tvam asi.* The Beloved is not merely the Such-ness of meditation. The Beloved is not merely the third person of the evolutionary impulse. The Beloved is the Infinity of Intimacy that knows your name, the Infinity of Intimacy that, as Barbara said:

> I said, *Thank you, God.* Then I heard a voice, and the voice said, *Thank you, Barbara.*

Maybe as we move into prayer, we can say with God's voice, *Thank you, Barbara.* Just, *thank you, Barbara,* in the voice of the Divine, *Thank you, Barbara.*

The Infinity of Intimacy that holds us says to every one of us, "Thank you, Barbara, with our name."

When we know that we are held by the Infinity of Intimacy and feel that thank you, Barbara, we are allowed to get excited in the Evolutionary Church. We're allowed to be Evangelicals. We don't have to hide our excitement.

We love Episcopalians but *Hello!* We're not doing Episcopalianism here. We're doing evolutionary evangelical delight! We're ecstatic! My friend Andrew calls it *ecstatic urgency.*

We're ecstatically urgent! And at the same time, we know that everything in our lives, our holy and broken *Hallelujah,* the dreams that were shattered, the relationships that fell apart, the pain and the trauma, all of it, is held by the Infinity of Intimacy.

The god you don't believe in doesn't exist.

God, the Infinity of Intimacy, who lives in third person as the evolutionary impulse, lives in first person in me, as me, and through me, and lives as second person—the same Beloved Barbara spoke of in the monastery every morning when she wrote in her some 200 journals:

> That Beloved is holding me now and receiving the holy and the broken *Hallelujah*!

EULOGY FOR BARBARA

Friends, we're entering now into the space that, Barbara, you and I joked about so many times, into the first space of it.

I can't even say the words.

It could not be that we would be eulogizing you! I mean Barbara, you were so not ready to go. You were not done. You were in your 90th year.

You were an evolutionary force of nature, and here we are about to speak your eulogy. I promised you an evolutionary party, so we're going to have a big evolutionary party eulogy.

But now we're in the church that you loved so much. Let me begin with a word from my teacher that we spoke about so many times, Dr. Soloveitchik.[3] He spoke about eulogy, and he drew deeply from the lineage of the mystics who said that eulogy is not a whitewash. Eulogy is not *pretty words* like Hafiz says when he mocks eulogy.

Eulogy is two things.

One: We ask your forgiveness, Barbara. We're here to ask your forgiveness for not having fully recognized you, not having fully seen you, and for

---

3   Dr. Soloveitchik typically refers to Rabbi Joseph B. Soloveitchik (1903–1993), one of the most influential Jewish thinkers and Talmudic scholars of the 20th century. He is often respectfully referred to as *The Rav* (The Rabbi) within Modern Orthodox Judaism.

somehow taking for granted that we could call you and that irrepressible, gorgeous, relentlessly alive, infinitely positive voice would always be there.

It's almost like we lived in this beautiful home on the ocean, but the ocean was just there. We stopped *seeing* you, so we ask for forgiveness.

Two: In the teaching of the mystics, in eulogy, in the days after Barbara passed, as her spirit is still in the continuity of consciousness (both fully with us and moving beyond the world in this moment), **there is the last opportunity in this lifetime to liberate the person who passed,** to liberate Barbara from loneliness.

To be lonely means to *not be able to take the lid off*, as Barbara would say to me and so many of you. We know the phrase. Barbara would say, "**I want to go the whole way in this lifetime.**"

Barbara was looking for the place to go the whole way. We're here to liberate you from loneliness. Yes, Barbara was lonely. We are all lonely in so many different ways. I want to start there because that's what we do in eulogy. We ask for forgiveness, and we move, Barbara, to see you.

EVOLUTIONARY LOVE CODE: LOVE IS A PERCEPTION

What's our code for today?

> To love is to know.
> Love's not merely an emotion.
> Love is a perception.
> Love means I see you.
> To be a lover is to see with God's eyes.

Barbara and I talked so often. What does it mean to be an Evolutionary Lover? An Evolutionary Lover is not sexual or romantic. An Evolutionary Lover is one who sees with God's eyes, who sees with Evolutionary eyes. So, we are here today, Barbara, to love you. We are here to know you with total humility.

It's the end of the code to know that also, in some deep way, you were *mystery*.

We love you in the unknowing, in the "cloud of unknowing," and we hold you with such reverence and such respect. Barbara, we want you to feel the respect, the infinite respect, that we are holding you in now.

I want to talk a few words about this continuity of consciousness. We are going to do it by capturing your consciousness in the best way we can, to liberate you from loneliness—in the tradition of the mystics—by recognizing you.

I'm going to start personally. Personally, I ask forgiveness for not being able to meet you in all the ways you wanted to be met. I did my best. We all did our best, but I know there were ways that I wasn't able to meet you. Please forgive me.

I speak for all of us here: my *I* is a *we* for any way that any of us, each of us individually, didn't call or didn't show up the way you might have wanted us to.

Oh my God! I want to talk about the gift that you gave all of us, in different ways, who worked closely with you. You gave us the gift of recognition. When I would speak to Barbara I felt fully recognized.

We are all lonely because we are systematically *mis-recognized*. Barbara was able to see someone and to be radically generous. Does everyone feel that in her recognition?

If we can say to Barbara now: *Thank you for recognizing me.*

When Barbara recognized you, you could rest. **Thank you, Barbara. Thank you for your generosity in recognizing us, in giving us a place to rest in full-hearted recognition.** When Barbara recognized you, there was nothing stingy. Barbara lived generously. It was a full-on, gorgeous recognition that you could hold.

That recognition that you received from Barbara would become the *strange attractor* for the rest of your life.

Thank you for recognizing us.

BARBARA WAS THE GOOD NEWS

We talked about Barbara as an Evolutionary Evangelical. Barbara *was* the Good News. But she was more than that. Barbara was also an Evolutionary Mystic in the truest term, but what Barbara sought to do was not to merge with the quality of eternity, the quality of be-ing. Barbara would seek to rest in *being*, which she loved to call *essence*, but Barbara sought to merge with the evolutionary impulse itself.

Where Barbara and I met was in this sentence: *I am evolution. I am evolution in person.*

I came to that sentence through the lineages, the lineage mystics, and Barbara came to it through Teilhard de Chardin, Bucky Fuller, Sri Aurobindo, and Jonas Salk. As we met in the *dharma*, that sentence was, *I am evolution in person.*

I ask and invite all of us, as Barbara's continuity of consciousness, if we can write, say, and feel together, *I am evolution in person*. I can't imagine anything making Barbara more ecstatic!

I am... and just feel that joy, Barbara.

Feel it and let it lift you up, love. Can you just let it lift you up? Can you receive that?

Oh my God! *I am...* Barbara, that's you! That's Barbara Marx Hubbard in front of you in the chat box—evolution in person. *I am evolution in person.*

Barbara Marx Hubbard, in the continuity of consciousness, Barbara, love, Barbara, you're with us. You're watching...

I AM EVOLUTION IN PERSON

Barbara, when you were evolution in person, it wasn't a phrase. You and I often did what we called "Holy of Holies." We would go to the Inside of the Inside, what you loved to call the heart of the hub of the wheel.

The heart of the hub of the wheel, the Holy of Holies, a word, a term, from Solomon's Temple in Jerusalem, the inside, the deepest of the deep. Wow!

In that place, we would talk about transformation. We would talk about very deep questions. We would talk about you, talk about your deep desire for the Blessing of the Father.

Louis Marx was your Dad, a toy tycoon, and on the 1955 cover of *Time* magazine.

Everyone's heard Barbara tell the story of being with President Eisenhower. Did you ever wonder why Barbara, at 16, was talking to President Eisenhower? Because Louis, her Dad, was a key financier and campaign person for Eisenhower and good friends with the president and all the generals.

So, Barbara grew up in this place, and she asked President Eisenhower, *What is the meaning of our power?*

But that story, where Barbara said, *Okay, now I want the blessing of the Father*, we tried to disambiguate; we tried to separate between what is the evolutionary impulse and what is the desire for the blessing of the Father.

We did that in your 90th year, and you said to me:

> Marc, I want to grow. I want to transform. Show me! Point out to me something that I cannot see, and I will transform it.

My friends, how many human beings at 30 say that? How many at 40?

> *Can you imagine the greatness of a human being who says, "I am evolution in person," not as a slogan, not merely as a declaration, but as the mandate of her own personal life?*

Barbara sought to transform every day. She never stopped evolving. She was utterly committed.

That's her radical commitment to Being. That's gorgeous! I've actually never seen it. I've never seen it in my entire life—where a person with world stature, with an ability to rest on her laurels, with so many important accomplishments, said, "No, no, no, I'm not getting older... I'm getting newer."

I AM GETTING NEWER

In the last four years we communicated, Barbara would meet me every single day, and **she would say, *I'm getting newer*, at least four times a day**, but often in long, complex, important letters.

She would tell with this gorgeous excitement lots of what we talked about yesterday but not because she was repeating it, not because she'd forgotten. She said she remembered very well that she said it. She was telling it to you again because she felt the newness of the day. She felt what she called *regenapause.*

She felt, *I'm completely renewed.* This day is utterly new, and I'm going to meet this day with all of my vitality and with all of my energy, and I'm going to take whatever fate throws at me today, and I'm going to transform it into destiny, and I'm going to be transformation.

Barbara was transformation.

When she said *getting newer* she would laugh. Everyone knows Barbara's particular laugh. I can't quite do it. I won't attempt Barbara, I promise! But it was this great laugh. When she would say something enormously serious, she would laugh. But she would laugh to punctuate that which had most gravitas. And as the feminine co-creator, her language, she would laugh just to open up some spacious space when she had said something incredibly profound.

Barbara had part of the liberation of loneliness that is the promise that the mystics give, and that we're giving to Barbara. It's our most valiant attempt at this moment, in our first eulogy. **Barbara was not radically positive because that was her nature.** She wasn't doing what our dear friend John Welwood[4] called a *spiritual bypass*.

Barbara wasn't spiritual bypassing. Barbara spoke about this in public many times. She spoke about her depression when she lived in Connecticut and how she went to a therapist. You've heard the story.

Barbara dealt with and engaged the emptiness. She engaged the void; she engaged depression throughout her entire life, not a clinical depression in the formal sense, but the sense of feeling the depth of the void.

Barbara wasn't radical positivity because it was a blithe cheeriness.

It wasn't a spiritual bypass.

Barbara actually faced the void every single day.

Barbara walked. Barbara never avoided (a-void-dance). Barbara walked through the void every single day in so many senses, but I want to add the ones that are unknown.

We can walk through the void like Barbara every single day.

---

4   John Welwood (March 12, 1943–January 17, 2019) was an American clinical psychologist, psychotherapist, teacher, and author, known for integrating psychological and spiritual concepts. He was the Director of the East/West Psychology Program at the California Institute of Integral Studies in San Francisco, and an associate editor of *Journal of Transpersonal Psychology*.

And Barbara understood the notion that to confess is not merely to confess your sins, but to confess your sins is just the beginning—actually, I confess my greatness.

Barbara confessed her greatness every day. Not as an egoic act—it wasn't an ego of declaration. It's what we would call here in Evolutionary Church a Unique Self declaration—a declaration of the personal face of the evolutionary impulse alive and awake as Barbara.

Barbara was unabashedly committed to her greatness, again in this most gorgeous way. **Barbara had a genuine humility; it was the humility of knowing that I can speak my greatness, and I'm committed to *modeling for people* what it means to go the whole way in this lifetime.**

I'm absolutely sure, Barbara, that I hear you whispering in my ear. So, I'm going to speak what Barbara asks to be said.

Barbara's awake, alive—the continuity of consciousness is happening right here, right now, in front of her.

IF YOU WANT TO KNOW THE ESSENCE OF BARBARA

Barbara, you were divine—you were divine in the sense of Barbara! You were the possibility of possibility. And Barbara just corrected me in my ear.

She said, *Marc, why are you saying "you were"?*

I apologize, Barbara. Again, Barbara, you *are* the possibility of possibility. Your continuity of consciousness lives with us in this moment.

And we see you, Barbara. We recognize you. And we love you, madly.

Do you know how Barbara would talk to everyone? I'm sure hundreds of people here have had that experience. She would hold your hand. She'd say, *Okay, hold my hand. Let's be together.* Then she'd shut her eyes. Like, wow.

Okay, number eight. The next quality of Barbara I want to point to is that **Barbara was not just a radical evolutionary, but Barbara actually lived**

in the eternity that resides in the moment. What do we mean by that? Barbara whispers in my ear, *Okay, explain to them, Marc, they didn't get what you meant.*

Here's the explanation. You remember having a conversation with Barbara? She'd sit with you. You might have been at a conference, at a convention.

You were sitting in a chair, and she'd enter into that conversation, and she would move to seduce you. When I say *seduce you*, I mean *to charm you*. Barbara and I laughed about this—not seduce you in an unholy way, to break your inappropriateness, to inappropriately break an appropriate boundary, but to seduce you in the language of the mystics.

To seduce you means to break the boundary of your smallness, to confess your greatness. The words of the *Song of Songs* (*Shir HaShirim* 1:4), which Barbara and I studied together—*mashkheni acharecha narutza*—Divinity seduces us to our greatness. Barbara seduced us to our greatness.

SHE CHARMED US

She charmed Bucky Fuller, but in the most beautiful sense of charm, the holy magical sense. She charmed Jonas Salk. She charmed her first husband, Earl, and her second husband, Sidney, who were so vital.

She charmed each one of these huge figures; she charmed me; she charmed all of you, but charmed in the most beautiful, holy, wondrous sense. She seduced us to our greatness in the fullness of her recognition.

So now, Barbara, now it's your turn, and we ask of you, the biggest gift you could give us now: let us, in this moment, liberate you from loneliness. Know that we see you, that we love you madly. And *the only way to be sane,* we would say to each other, *is to love madly.*

To love is to know, and to know is to love. We feel you, and we feel your presence, alive.

What's the deepest confession you can make? Friends, what's the deepest confession you can make?

So, Barbara and I developed, in the last couple of years, the Wheel 2.0. Barbara first gorgeously conceived of this with John Whiteside. John sketched it on a napkin at a restaurant, Barbara told me, this Wheel of Co-Creation, which is this gorgeous tool for social synergy. And social synergy is just another word for intimacy.

So, as Barbara would say it, *How do we join needs and resources to create a larger intimacy, a larger social synergy that can unleash the full creative potential that can take us through the 11th hour across the precipice?* That's Barbara.

We created a Wheel of Co-Creation 2.0 on another napkin, over lunch in Portland. We were drinking wine. Everyone knows Barbara loved wine at about four o'clock in the afternoon, right? She would have two, three glasses, completely unfazed; I would have two sips, and I couldn't get any farther!

At the heart of the hub of the wheel we placed together, *desire*. Desire. We've exiled desire to its beautiful, but merely sexual expression.

But, for the evolutionary mystics, when the unmanifest manifests Reality and says, *Yes*, that's a desire. The desire is not just to revisit the past, not just the eternity of the present. **The desire is to invoke the memory of the future.**

And Barbara, you were an evolutionary throw forward. You were a memory of the future. You incarnated that. We put at the heart of the hub of the wheel *desire*, and we developed a practice, which is, also at the heart of the hub of the wheel 2.0. It is to confess your greatness by knowing your heart's desire.

Here Barbara would add something critical. She would say it in her language; I say it in different language. It's the same but *feel* Barbara's words here. It's so gorgeous:

19

Your heart's desire, your yearning.

Barbara thought, *I'm in Lakeland, Connecticut. I'm restless. I'm wanting more.* I realized that's not pathology—that can't be solved by recovering the memory of the past. My yearning is the divine yearning.

My heart's desire is the *divine desire,* not *any* desire, not pseudo-desire, not pseudo-eros, but my deepest heart's desire.

My deepest heart's desire is God's desire. That's Barbara's.

She was so excited about that, so we placed *desire* at the heart of the hub of the wheel, and we joined genius.

JOINING GENES TO JOINING GENIUS

Barbara was madly excited about moving from her phrase, *joining genes,* to *joining genius.*

To move from joining genes to joining genius means that we actually access and hold together a shared desire and a completely different set of teachings in a different language.

Before I met Barbara and merged joining genes to joining genius, we spoke of the move from *role mate* to *soul mate* to *whole mate.*

- ◆ Role mate: We're raising the kids. We're raising the family to survive and thrive.
- ◆ Soul mate: We look deeply into each other's eyes, and we begin to see each other. To love is to know.
- ◆ Whole mate: To be a whole mate means not just I look deeply in your eyes, and it's not just about personal fulfillment. Whole mate is when we look together at a shared horizon.

Whole mate means we don't just look at each other and see each other.

Anyone who knows Barbara—and we all know Barbara here, and we're all loving you madly —know that Barbara lived whole mate-ness.

To love is to know is not just to love, it is to know you. It's not just the story of your wounds and the story of your trauma, but to love is to know. To be a whole mate is to be in service of the whole, together—to join genius, not just to procreate, join genes.

Barbara's phrase, to join genius, to co-create. To move in our shared expression from role mate to soul mate to whole mate.

Barbara's greatest passion was this realization, and we must have talked about this a thousand times and beautifully each time. Each time was new because *we got newer* each time. The passion that drives human beings to come together in sexuality is transcended and included, but sometimes just transcended. We leave sexuality behind.

With my brother, as brothers, as sisters, fathers and sons, mothers and daughters, friends—we can become whole mates beyond sexuality to what I call *Eros*, what Barbara calls *supra-sexuality*. **Supra-sexual co-creation means I'm a *whole mate*.**

We're not merely joining genes at all, right? There's overpopulation—an explosion.

We need to join geniuses in the passion to join geniuses to co-create.

We'll actually unleash the infinite potential and creativity of the human being to look into the face of the abyss and take us to the next level. **We'll birth the new human and the new humanity.**

We're going to close with this last thought, offering, and prayer. We're going to pray, and then we're going to come back and close.

Let's open our hearts. Can we open our hearts? Can we just totally, completely, open our hearts?

We can just meditate with Barbara and on Barbara in the best way we can.

Barbara, Barbara, you were a blazing light in this world. The wild stallions that moved you were yokes to the evolutionary impulse itself.

Evolution, Barbara, was awake and is awake as you in person.

Reality delighted and delights in having a Barbara experience in the continuity of consciousness.

Barbara, you felt the ecstatic urgency of the evolutionary impulse moving through you all the time.

Barbara, you took the pain of the void and turned it into the joy of evolutionary activism. You took fate, and you turned it into destiny time and again and again.

Barbara, you were the greatest evolutionary storyteller of our time.

Barbara, you dreamed of social synergy, of the peace room, of the Office for the Future. You incarnated a vice-presidential bid, a historic speech at the Democratic National Convention.

You were the great fount, speaking the word of conscious evolution.

All of these were vehicles that you audaciously and creatively manifested for the impulse and as the impulse.

Abraham Maslow, Bucky Fuller, Jonas Salk, and so many more, including this writer and so many of you listening—you charmed us all.

You recognized us all.

You inspired us all.

You called us forth with you.

Friends, in this moment, let's feel it together. Let's know it together.

And the continuity of consciousness is true.

We are with you now, Barbara.

One heart—our heart is with your heart.
One love—our love is with your love.
One desire—our desire is with your desire.

Barbara, you're surrounded
and held in radical evolutionary intimacy.

We are together!

THERE MAY BE A TIME, BUT THIS IS NOT THAT DAY

Yes, there are those who say that there may be a time when *Homo sapiens* turn their attention from each other and lose themselves in the *illusion* of separation when death triumphs, **but this is not *that* day**, friends. **This day—we are *with* you in this day.** We are celebrating your life. We are recognizing you. *We are inspired by you.* We're honoring your deepest intention of the LoveIntelligence for all of us to find our heart's desire.

Yes, Barbara, you spoke about the possible dystopia, love. There may be a time when *Homo sapiens* descend into dystopia and we forget that we're the LoveIntelligence of the Cosmos, evolution in person. **But this is not *that* day.**

We're with you, Barbara. We're inspired by you. We are impacted by you.

We're holding you in the evolutionary integrity and delight of all of our holy time together, each one of us.

Yes, there are those who say that there may be a day when we forget that we live in a world of outrageous pain, and the only response is Outrageous Love. But my friends, **this is not *that* day.**

Most importantly, this is the day in which we introduce the new human and the new humanity: *Homo amor universalis* and *Homo amor*.

Barbara and I spoke about this almost every day. Our friend, Yuval Harari, wrote about *homo deus*, who bio-hacks his way to immortality and most of humanity becomes… not exploited, but irrelevant.

Barbara, Zak, and I talked about *Homo amor*. We birthed *Homo amor* together. Barbara used to call it *Homo universalis*. I called it *Homo amor*.

One day, we spoke right before church. We said, let's call it *Homo amor universalis*. And then several weeks later, we said, you know what? It's *Homo amor*.

Homo amor answers the question: *Who are you?*

Who are you? I am Homo amor!

That was Barbara's greatest dream, and her next years were dedicated and committed to articulating it together, and we're going to do it together still. Barbara, myself, and every single one of us here. **All of us together are going to birth *Homo amor*—evolution in person.** *Homo amor* asks and responds to a very important question.

The question is, *who are you?*

Who are you? I am *Homo amor*. But what does it mean to be *Homo amor*?

Homo amor knows that answer to the question of who are you: *You are the irreducibly unique expression.*

Barbara, you know, every word we did together. Let's say this together:

> You are the irreducibly unique expression of the LoveIntelligence and LoveBeauty that is the initiating and animating Eros and energy of All-That-Is; that lives in you, as you, and through you; that never was, is, or will be ever again—other than through your heart's desire.

When you confess your greatness and find your deepest heart's desire, you're able to access *your unique perspective* and *give your unique gift*, which is desperately needed to address a unique need in your unique circle of intimacy and influence that can be addressed by no one that ever was, is, or will be—other than you alone.

Whenever we got to this point, Barbara would add: "and you write your name in the noosphere as you confess your greatness and give your gift, which is your deepest heart's desire."

Barbara, we love you. Barbara, we love you madly. Feel our love. We miss you.

WE GO TO PRAYER

Barbara, we're going to pick up the torch. We're going to light the world on fire with *Homo amor*.

I wanna know what love is. We're going to take and sing those words as we do every week—as you asked me to, Barbara—as a prayer.

"I Wanna Know What Love Is" — Foreigner [See Appendix]

Evolutionary Love in person. Oh my god. We end with a prayer for Barbara. We are Barbara.

Barbara, you are inspiring us. You're lighting us up, to feel and hear these words, and we're going to bring it all together. *Barbara, you inspire me.*

We are Barbara. Barbara, you inspire me. Thank you, Barbara.

- I love you. Evolutionary Love. All the way up and all the way down.
- Barbara, you inspire me. Thank you, Barbara, right? I love you. And let the tears flow, and we miss you.

You're with us, and the continuity of consciousness is true. And a visionary has left us, but we're going to see with your eyes, Barbara. Thank you, Barbara. I love you.

You're awake and alive with us right here. We're joining genius to co-create. *Homo amor* is live.

Barbara, thank you, Barbara.

This moment's never going to come again, so if you're in the bleachers, if you're in the stands, and if you're kind of going to make the day—step out of the stands and get on the court and speak that word to Barbara so she can feel it, and you can lift Barbara, as the mystics say, like a prayer to the sky.

Pour energy into her. Pour energy into you, beloved Barbara, for this next stage of your journey. And stay with us, please, and we release you. You are free, be liberated, to go wherever your heart's desire is. Barbara, we are in devotion to your heart's desire.

But friends, don't miss the last moment just to tell Barbara. There's not going to be another moment like this ever. **This moment is an eternity in time. It's a new moment.** It never was before; it never will be again. Barbara, you are free. You are free. Follow your heart's desire. We love you.

"How Could Anyone" — Libby Roderick [See Appendix]

We end church with this, like we do every week. This was your favorite part of church, right? And you always forgot to ask for a contribution. We're not going to ask for a contribution this week.

The contribution is all of us coming together and being here. And we look in each other's eyes and we say, *how could anyone...*

> *How could anyone ever tell you*
> *you were anything less than beautiful?*
> *How could anyone ever tell you*
> *you were less than whole?*
> *How could anyone fail to notice*
> *that our love . . .*

. . . all of us together with you, Barbara, our love affair with you is nothing less than a miracle—

> *How deeply you're connected to my soul?*

Oh my God, Barbara, we have confessed your greatness. **You inspire us, you're with us, you're alive.** We're going to light the world on fire with *Homo amor.*

Thank you, Barbara. We love you madly.

Amen.

CHAPTER TWO

RESURRECTION AND RENEWAL: RECLAIMING LOVE IN EVOLUTIONARY CHURCH

Episode 132 — April 20, 2019

BARBARA, YOU ARE ALIVE HERE IN CHURCH WITH US

Before we begin, I want to invoke my beloved evolutionary partner, whole mate, Barbara. And Barbara, with your permission, beloved—turn to you directly as I've tried to this week and just invite you into the church that has been your home and will continue to be your home.

Oh, my God, when you passed, Barbara, you weren't ready, and we weren't ready.

I am looking, friends, at my phone right now. And I want to read you something, a text that I got from Barbara just hours before. And it was this beautiful set of texts that we had going back and forth. **She said, "Wow, the church of Evolutionary Love, this is my home, this is my place, I'm so excited, this is our future."**

And then she starts talking about medical issues. And then she said, "I'm going to live." At the bottom, she says,

"Feeling encouraged, I'm going to live"—with three thousand thank yous and heart, heart, heart....

"Feeling encouraged that I'm going to live." And the answer is, "Barbara, you are absolutely right, you are going to live, and you are alive, and you are with us." You are both in a realm beyond us and in your passing—we learned again, in this way that was kind of unimaginable, in a new way, because there's no death that's the same as any other death. We know all about death, but when we encounter it so closely, with someone so close to the fabric of our hearts—and Barbara, if there was anyone we thought would live forever, it was you.

If there was anyone we couldn't quite imagine—and of course, we should have thought, *Wow, you're in your 90th year.*

But then you weren't here. We realized again that the veneer between the two worlds is so thin, the slipstream into the next world is right there. And at the same time, you are absolutely committed with us, and you are alive here in church as you were with us, as we speak, and as we share the *dharma* that we articulated together.

As I share I'm resonating it as Marc and as Barbara. All of us share in the chat box. **Barbara, we're all Barbara. We're all our Unique Self, and we're also Barbara. You're living in us, and we're living in you.**

I remember, Barbara, the words that I shared with you about the moment when I decided to become a teacher. My teacher had passed away, and I was 16 years old. You remember the story, love. It was in the middle of the big *Purim* party. *Purim* is the carnival holiday in the Hebrew tradition. I was 16, and he was 32, and he fell down and passed. He had an aneurysm. Again, like you, although completely different age, no preparation.

The dean of the school, because I was very close to my teacher, asked me to do the eulogy. So, I did, and I cited a passage from the Talmud that says *ma zar'o b'chaim af hu b'chaim*[5]—if a person lives on through their spirit and impacts those they are beloved to, then they are fully and radically alive.

Yes, there are many mystical realms where we can do a soul ascent, and you go to the next worlds in the interior traditions. Let's go in the most simple and basic way.

> *As long as Barbara's impacting us,*
> *as long as we're hearing her laugh,*
> *she's with us forever.*

That's why we've kept Barbara's picture; we always want to see her picture in church. We want to see your smile, Barbara, and feel your delight. We want to feel your resonance.

On the one hand, you want us to play without you as we played with you. You want us to go on fully alive, fully engaged, and fully building this Evolutionary Church to the vision that we held together, for the Church which has millions of people all around the world, all sorts of Evolutionary Church ministers all over the world.

And there's One-World Church, all over the world, and it's a cascading wave of Outrageous Love responding to outrageous pain. It is the self-organizing universe in person as the Evolutionary Church creating the social change, creating the transformation that we need in this eleventh hour of humanity.

And the church, like the Gospel Church of the Black community in the 1960s, becomes the agent of the civil rights and the global rights of the new story that transforms humanity.

- ♦ We are in Bethlehem.
- ♦ We are da Vinci in Florence.

---

5 Babylonian Talmud, Tractate Ta'anit 5b.

- We are marching in Selma. We are marching together and creating as we march, not a war room, but a peace room, where peace can transform Reality.

Barbara, you are with us, and we hear your voice.

And of course, we'll be mentioning you all the time. And we'll be talking to you. And we'll be talking about you in the past tense, and we'll be talking about you in the present tense.

Barbara, you were right when you said, the last words you wrote to me were, "I'm going to live."

And then you wrote three bowing hands and eight hearts. You were absolutely right, you are going to live. You are here with us, and we're here with you—with tears in my eyes. And welcome, Barbara, to church this morning.

We're so wildly delighted to be with you. And aren't you happy? We're going to build this church together. *Mine eyes have seen the glory of the coming of the Lord.* Sometimes I would call Barbara at night, and it was a phrase she loved. She would finish church and text me to say, "My eyes have seen the glory." So, Barbara, here we are.

We're entering into church week 132. Thirty-two in Hebrew is *lev*, heart. This is the week of heart. We're on the Saturday before the Resurrection in the Christian tradition. We're going to be talking about that. For those of you who did a *Seder*, which was also the last supper in the Christian tradition, the Passover *Seder* happened all over the world last night.

We bring all the traditions together in a larger whole and a larger lineage, the lineage of Evolutionary Love.

Oh, my God, what do we do in the Evolutionary Church? This church, that's the One-World Church, this cascading force of transformation. **We're reclaiming the codes of Reality.** We are writing the Evolutionary Love Codes of *Homo amor*.

My friend, Yuval Harari wrote a book *Homo Deus* which sold millions and millions of copies. It's a tragic book, a book without a story. It's a book about the wealthy bio-hacking their way to immortality.

It's a book about a potential case coming into the world where, going forward, those who are wealthy—those who can afford augmentation, all the gene fixing and gene splicing, who can afford to recreate themselves in this new vision of future technology—will become a small elite on planet Earth.

You'll have this huge group—a massive majority who can't afford that— which will reintroduce a kind of *Hunger Games*, dystopian, *Blade Runner*, caste system on planet Earth.

We're confined to a *Homo deus*, this human being who's desperately grasping for longevity and immortality—but who's lost any sense of the infinite value of the eternity that resides in the moment—of the utter glory that it means to be a human being. **We're living in a world without a story, we're living in a world without a narrative, without a shared vision. What we're doing here in Evolutionary Church is reclaiming that vision.**

I hear the phone ringing, and that must be God calling to say, "Oh, my God, you are doing a good job, folks. We need Evolutionary Church." And we need the Evolutionary Church to tell the story.

To tell the story, we need to reintroduce and reclaim the core characters in the story.

At the center of the story is the human being, and at the center of the story is God.

NOT JUST *TAT TVAM ASI* OR THE INFINITY OF POWER, GOD IS ALSO THE INFINITY OF INTIMACY

God lives in us, but God doesn't *only* live in us. It's not *just* that we are, as Dante says, a *baby-faced Divine*. God also holds us. As Rumi said, *We fall into the arms of the beloved*. Our beloved, Barbara, would write every morning to the Beloved. God is not just the Infinity of Power that courses through the Cosmos, God in the third person.

> *God is not just tat tvam asi, Thou art That, the God who lives in me. God is not just the Infinity of Power. God is the Infinity of Intimacy. And friends, can we rest for a second until billions of people around the world realize this?*

And that's our mission in the Evolutionary Church: The god you don't believe in doesn't exist, the cosmic vending machine god, where you put in a quarter and get a new car. The god who:

- Is owned by one religion
- Punishes you for self-pleasuring
- Tells you that if you eat this or eat that, you might go to hell
- Is divorced from the world, who only lives outside of the world
- Says that there's no creativity in the world and who demands only obedience
- Is merely an impersonal evolutionary force, that's not sufficient: *the small god*

Abraham Kook—the great erotic mystic whom Barbara and I studied together in the Holy of Holies—Kook said that *you've got to be a heretic.*

The great believers are heretics, meaning they denied the smallness of God. **There's heresy which is faith, and there's faith which is heresy.** We need to have the heresy that's faith.

We realize that God is the first person in me, the third person Force in Cosmos, and the Infinity of Intimacy that loves me madly.

If there is an intimate moment that we have between us, that intimacy participates in the larger Field of Intimacy. Does everyone get that?

When I yearn for intimacy, that's the Divine within me yearning for intimacy. We live in an Intimate Universe, the way Solomon, the great lineage master, says it in the great Song of Solomon, *tocho ratzuf ahava*, which means: *it's insides are lined with intimacy; it's insides are lined with love.* That Infinity of Intimacy has a personal face and says to each of us:

- How are you this morning?
- How are you doing?
- I hear every thought, gesture, impulse, pain, beauty, and poignancy, that is you.

In *Walden*, Thoreau says, *there may be people who live lives of quiet desperation*, but actually, there are no lives of lonely desperation—**we're never lonely in our desperation because we're always held by the Infinity of Intimacy.**

THE INFINITY OF INTIMACY CARRIES US IN EVERY SECOND

Do you all remember that story that became famous all over the world that comes from an original, mystical group? It comes originally from the Hasidic tradition of Hebrew mysticism, and it got retold. Tell it with me, together.

> It's a story about a man walking along the beach. He looks to find his footprints in the sand, and he looks next to them and

sees another set of footprints in the sand because the Infinity of Intimacy, God, is always walking with us.

But then he gets into trouble, life gets hard, and there's crucifixion. It's the Saturday before Easter, the moment of darkness, uncertainty, and loss. It's the moment when we've confronted death before the Resurrection, and walking along the beach he looks behind him and sees only one set of footprints and he's devastated. Where did you go, God?

And we look behind us and see only one set of footprints, and he raises his voice and says, *Oh my God, where did you go? And now, you abandon me.*

A voice emerges from deep within the depths and the voice emerges from on high. Do you know what the voice says? The voice says, *"No, no, no, at this moment there's only one set of footprints because I'm carrying you. I'm carrying you, and those footprints are mine."*

My friends, the Infinity of Intimacy is carrying us in every moment.

And that's not the dogmatic god; it's not the god that's imposed. **We have a realization, the same way we realize in meditation, that God lives within.** We realize in prayer, as Rumi, Hafiz, Theresa of Avila, Luria, and as all the great mystics in the generation with the most subtle and speculative minds—doing the experiments of interior science—realized:

- ◆ We are held.
- ◆ We are never alone.
- ◆ There is never lonely desperation.

So, in this moment we go before the Infinity of Intimacy, and we fall on our knees. Because every time we're on our knees, we're on our knees before God, we're in the Infinity of Intimacy. Whenever we're broken, we bring to

God our holy and broken *Hallelujah*, and we say, *Lift me up and carry me.* And God never says *no.*

That's the prayer that God/Goddess, the Infinity of Intimacy, always says: *Yes.* In this moment, we reclaim God in the Evolutionary Love Codes. In this new and higher consciousness, we bring our holy and broken *Hallelujah* before the Divine. *Amen.*

EVOLUTIONARY LOVE CODE: THERE IS NO EROS WITHOUT GNOSIS

More than confessing your sins, you must confess your greatness, and your greatness is your heart's desire.

To confess your greatness is to confess your heart's desire.

To confess your heart's desire, you must know yourself.

To know yourself, you must love yourself. There is no knowledge without love, and there is no love without knowledge.

There is no gnosis without Eros; there is no Eros without gnosis.

Love is not merely a human experience. Love is not merely the human experience of an emotion. Love is a perception.

Love is a perception identification complex. Love is an epistemological act which reveals ontology.

To love is to know, and to know is to love. And yet, there is no love without unknowing.

There is no unknowing without love.

To love God is to know God.

To love God is to love God in the unknowing.

We are in the Saturday before Easter and the first day of Passover. In Christianity, it's called the tomb of metamorphosis. I want to just take a few minutes to weave together our code, to weave together Passover and Easter.

What does our code say? Our code says, *we've got to confess our greatness.*

More than confessing your sins, you must confess your greatness.

And your greatness is your deepest heart's desire.

To confess your greatness is to confess your heart's desire.

To confess your heart's desire, you must know yourself, and to know yourself is to love yourself.

There is no love without knowledge. There is no knowledge without love.

So, let's be with this. I was on a beautiful call a little while ago, and there was a lot of feeling. But it was actually missing knowledge. It was missing *dharma.* And lots of the New Age world is a beautiful world, but *it's filled with a lot of feeling, without distinctions, without knowledge.* And then, sometimes we have science that's doing knowledge but disowns the love that's driving it. **We need to bring love and knowledge together.**

Love without knowledge is dangerous.
And knowledge without love is dangerous.

The *hieros gamos*, the divine marriage, is love and knowledge.

Now, what's Passover? In Hebrew, Passover is called *Pesach.* The great mystics of the *Merkabah*, the great mystics of the chariot, in Hebrew mysticism said that *Pesach* is *the mouth that talks.*

And what do you do at the Last Supper, which was the Passover *Seder*? As we weave together in the One World Church all the great traditions into this larger whole, greater than the sum of the parts.

What do you do at the Passover *Seder*? So, simply, historically, we remember that the Hebrews left Egypt. Why do we care about that? Why do we care about a historical event from 4,000 years ago? Because, my friends, **what that event means is a rejection of the status quo:** *We think we're slaves,* *and we're going to be slaves forever.* The great mystical texts say that no one ever left Egypt. A slave born in Egypt was a slave whose children, grandchildren, and great-great grandchildren would all be slaves in Egypt. No!

- ◆ In steps the force of healing and transformation.
- ◆ In steps the God/Goddess.
- ◆ In steps history that moves toward transformation.

And the status quo is shattered.

And the greatest slave driver in the world is the belief that yesterday determines today.

Friends, can we say that *dharma*?

The greatest slave driver in the world is the belief that yesterday determines today.

Yesterday does not determine today. I can actually be free today. I can become free in this moment. I am born free in this moment. Are we willing to be born free?

I say to myself, *Marc, all the patterns that I couldn't overcome yesterday, on Good Friday—today, on this Saturday, I'm going to overcome.*

When I'm born free today, what can we do, my friends? What can we do when we're born free today?

We can find our heart's desire and confess our greatness. And I want to invite everyone—and again, I'm sorry, but this week there's just tears in my eyes because of Passover, Easter, Barbara, this new moment. This new moment when the sun has set, and the sun is rising again.

I want to ask everyone to do a special kind of, if it pleases your heart— together, can we confess our greatness? I confess my greatness. Here's a word. I confess my greatness. And the Evolutionary Church is mine to build. It's not Marc's to build; it's ours to build. So, if we can say and I know it's a lot to write: *I confess my greatness.*

I confess my greatness, and the Evolutionary Church is ours to build. This is ours, this is our church.

The center of the church is our community; it's the dharma. It's not Marc, and it's not Barbara. It's why the church can go on without Barbara; the church will go on without Marc one day.

I confess my greatness—my greatness is needed here, my contribution and my presence.

REALITY MOVES TOWARDS RESURRECTION

Now friends, let's go to the next step: Easter. From Passover to Easter. Easter is this moment of resurrection. And what does Easter say? Easter says that out of every shattering, new light will be born. We experienced a shattering ten days ago, but new light is being born.

And is there anyone that can stand up and say:

- "My friends, I have never experienced a shattering?"
- "My friends, I have never been broken?"
- "I have never betrayed?"
- "I have never fallen into a well of sadness where I was paralyzed by fear and grief?"

Is there someone here who has not in some sense experienced crucifixion? **We've all experienced crucifixion.** I've done enough for a few people, just in case anyone was missing and I can make it up.

> *We've all experienced darkness, but we know that Reality is moving towards resurrection. And we are all the Christs, and the Christ lives in us.*

And the Christ is the One Love that is lifting me higher.
And the Christ is the answer to, *I want to know what love is.*
And the Christ is the Buddha and Lao Tzu.
And the Christ is secular humanism.
And the Christ is *Homo amor.*

WE ARE *HOMO AMOR* MOVING TOWARDS RESURRECTION

We are at a moment as we stand between dystopia and utopia where we are telling a new story, and we are becoming the new human. We are becoming the new species, and we are *Homo amor.* Christ is not one Jesus—Christ is *Homo amor.* And *Homo amor* is moving toward resurrection.

So, we are *Homo amor.* We are moving towards resurrection. Reality moves toward resurrection. Can we find that: We are *Homo amor* moving toward resurrection.

Friends, *Homo amor* and *Homo amor universalis* are two names for the same. Barbara and I exchanged, had a deep talk, and we decided to use the word *Homo amor* as the major word because we want to be able to respond to *Homo Deus,* but I'll move between them. And we move between them a lot.

Someone had asked the question, "Where is *universalis*?" and said, "Let's be *Homo amor universalis*." Barbara and I sat and talked about it, and we said that *Homo amor* includes *universalis* and has the whole story. So, thank you for asking the question.

We are Homo amor moving toward resurrection. We've been shattered, we've had holy and broken Hallelujahs, and we've made mistakes and fallen. But yesterday doesn't determine today.

The only slave driver—says Passover—is that yesterday determines today. Today is a new world, and in this world, I am born free. And in this world I am not alone. I am being carried. I am being carried and we together as Evolutionary Church—with Barbara, with every single one of us—today's a new world.

We are committed here in Evolutionary Church not just to ourselves, not just to church, but Evolutionary Church is the vehicle—the *Merkavah*, the chariot—for the transformation and the healing of Reality, for telling the new story for the evolution of love, for the next step in conscious evolution.

We are born free today, and we can answer the great question of *how deep is your love?* Our love is so deep, our love is getting deeper every second, and we can dance it and rejoice in it. So, Barbara in heaven and us below. **And this is the place where heaven and earth kiss.**

CHAPTER THREE

MORE THAN CONFESSING YOUR SINS, YOU MUST CONFESS YOUR GREATNESS

Episode 133 — April 27, 2019

REALITY IS A SET OF HABITS

I'm going to set the intention; we will resonate our code and in we go. The order of service is very important. The reason we put an order of service in church—and Barbara Marx Hubbard and I talked about this all the time—is because there's a difference between spontaneity that happens in a part of a ritual dance and spontaneity that happens by itself.

When you want to transform your character, when you want to evolve the source code, when you want to transform humanity, when we stand between dystopia and utopia, when we need to participate directly in the evolution of love—there's only one move: the move is always to re-habituate.

Reality is a set of habits. There are cosmic habits of the Cosmos, and there are personal habits. Everything happens because water drips on a rock, and when it drips, and it drips, and drips, ultimately the regularity, the steadiness of the habit is what forms and transforms.

Now, we look at a habit as something we can't break: *a bad habit.* We identify habits with bad habits, but that's not quite right.

My colleague and friend, Stephen Covey, when he wrote his book *Seven Habits of Highly Effective People,* was coming from a Mormon background. But he understood practice. What spiritual practice is about is regularly practicing a set of new habits.

OUR INTENTION IS TO PARTICIPATE IN THE EVOLUTION OF LOVE

If you want to understand what we're doing in church:

- We're opening the door.
- We're getting into the source code.
- We're bypassing ego.
- We're accessing Outrageous Love and stepping inside.

We're on the inside. We establish insight, we code; we're doing a re-code of Reality. **We access the Evolutionary Love Codes in order to fulfill our intention, which is no less than the healing and transformation of planet Earth so that we'll be here for another generation.**

---

*Our intention is to participate
in the evolution of love.*

Setting our intention is now going to become a regular part of service. Let's all set our intentions together. We're not just here for ourselves alone. We're here for ourselves, honoring our dignity and our Infinite Personhood.

- But we're here to participate in the evolution of love.
- We're here to participate in the evolution of culture and consciousness and to do it in a very particular way.
- We're here to write the new story.

This is what da Vinci did when you couldn't go into every village that was decimated by suffering beyond imagination. Through the Black Death that ravaged Europe, through poverty and various forms of caste systems and degradation, da Vinci realized the way to stand on the abyss of darkness and say *let there be light* was to tell the new story, to tell the news for what was the story of modernity:

- It was the story of human rights.
- It was the story from which feminism emerged.
- It was the story that abolished slavery in a period of about a hundred years, which all the great religions didn't manage to do.

Da Vinci, in that threshold point between premodernity and postmodernity, told a new story which introduced modern medicine and technology. We're now at this threshold point—or juncture point like they say in Systems Theory—after modernity and postmodernity; we've deconstructed all the old values, and we haven't adopted anything in their place. There's no reconstructive project.

And so, we're all talking to each other, we're all interconnected, we're all Facebooking, but we have a fragile infrastructure. **We're faced by ten major existential threats, and we have no idea who we are.** And so, in order to do what da Vinci did, we have to actually invoke a new Renaissance.

To invoke a new Renaissance is to awaken the new human and the new humanity; it's *Homo amor*. We are here as *Homo amor*, who brings together in him/herself the *universalis* dimension, the high-tech dimension of the mass power. And *Homo amor* brings together the interior realization that *I am a unique configuration of Evolutionary Love,* and *I have the power of the Roman gods.*

Homo amor, I'm a unique expression of the LoveIntelligence. I'm an Outrageous Lover committing acts of love. And we stand against that vision of *Homo Deus* that my friend, Yuval Harari, put out not as an ideal, but as the disaster: *The Hunger Games* dystopia in which only the wealthy augment, and only the wealthy get direct access to machine learning, robotics and artificial intelligence. And most of the jobs in the world within 30 years are supposed to be obsolete.

We now have two castes. We have a kind of super caste right now—*Homo Deus*—who bio-hacks their way to some form of immortality. Then the rest of the world is jobless because jobs have become obsolete. But they have no place, no vision, no purpose. Think of *Hunger Games*, if you want to think of a movie. We're 30 years away from something like that.

We're at a pivoting point, and the most important thing we can do is to tell a new story.

What's the new story? It's the story of *Homo amor*. That's our intention, and we're going to reset it every week. We are Outrageous Lovers participating in the evolution of love, and every week we enter into an Evolutionary Love Code, to lay it down, to open it up, to love it open.

We are excited, we are evangelicals. As Barbara Marx Hubbard and I always said: *We're not embarrassed to be excited, but bring in the Good News.* Not dogmatic news; no dogma here. It's **dharma at the best integration of the deepest insights pre-modern, modern, and postmodern, woven into a greater story.**

Holding humbly all the uncertainty, holding humbly all that we don't know, holding humbly the mystery, and yet, audaciously standing at the abyss of darkness and suffering and saying *yes, we're going to create a better tomorrow.* Yes, it is us, *yes we are the evolution of love.*

THE WORLD NEEDS A STORY ABOUT THE EVOLUTIONARY LOVE THAT ANIMATES EVERYTHING

This is our Church, but this is our Church of evolution. I love it, and this is the revolution: **We're going to light the world aflame with *Homo amor*.**

- We are in Bethlehem.
- We are in the Good News.
- We are in Venice.
- We are Outrageous Lovers, and we have to be outrageous.

What the world needs more than anything else at this moment in time is a story that tells us that that which unites us is so much greater than that which divides us.

The world needs a story which doesn't widen the gap between the have and the have-nots, a story which is a story about the *Amor*, the Evolutionary Love that animates us uniquely and that drives and animates everything.

And one of the things that my beloved whole mate, Barbara Marx Hubbard, would say all the time was that *evolution always moves to higher levels of freedom, consciousness, and order.* And I would add on *elegant* order. It's not going to stop now.

That was the radical *yes* that Barbara Marx Hubbard felt, that I feel, that we feel, resonating in us, this unrelenting positivity. But that *yes* is because, and here are the words of the ancient wisdom master Solomon, *tocho ratzuf ahava,*[6] its insides are lined with love—Reality is a love story. It's got a lot of agony, and it's got a lot of ecstasy. But if you don't understand that Reality

---

6 Song of Songs (Shir HaShirim) 3:10.

is an Intimate Universe, *Universe: A Love Story*, then you can't even engage evil.

Because why shouldn't there be evil? Why shouldn't there be suffering? If it's just a material, reductionist world, which makes absolutely no sense, which is a product of *oops*, well then, why wouldn't there be brutal suffering in the world?

It's only when I understand that its insides are lined with love—that Reality is amor—that I can awaken as Outrageous Love, feeling Outrageous Love pulsing uniquely through me, and I know that I have unique Outrageous Acts of Love to commit that no one who ever was or is will do but me.

GOD IS THE INFINITY OF INTIMACY INTO WHOSE ARMS I FALL IN EVERY MOMENT

Today we're going to talk about how I access my heart's desire, confess my greatness, and know which Outrageous Acts of Love are mine to commit.

But first we're about to go into prayer and listen to Leonard Cohen, who now works with us full-time. After he passed onto the next world he was looking for a church. And he said: *I'm going to hang out in the church of Evolutionary Love. That is where the future is, and that is where the memory of the future is, and that is where people are scanning for evolving the source code, and that is where da Vinci is, and that's where people are Outrageous Lovers.*

Leonard is going to resonate our hymn, singing the holy and the broken *Hallelujah*, as we move into prayer.

Then when we turn to prayer, we are on our knees, and we're always on our knees.

We're standing tall and proud, we're taking a stand—and we're on our knees at the same time.

+ We are the first person of the Divine.

48

- ◆ We are the evolutionary impulse.
- ◆ We are touched by *tat tvam asi*.
- ◆ We are that we are.
- ◆ We are the coursing Outrageous Love that moves the sun and other stars.

And yet in every moment we are held.

We've lost that conversation with God. We've lost the notion that God's not only within us. God's not only—She's not only—breathing us, but She's also holding us.

Remember Rumi and Hafiz, those great Sufi poets, the great *Kabbalists*, and the Kashmir Shaivite masters? Oh, my God, *every place you fall, you fall into Her hands.* She's the Mother, She's the Lover, She's the Lover of the Song of Songs. She knows us personally and intimately but not as a cosmic vending machine, ethnocentric, homophobic, punishing, personal, metaphor, grandfather/grandmother in the sky god with a long beard. And grandma with a beard, that's pretty frightening. Not that kind of personal god, but God who is the Personhood of Cosmos.

God is the personhood of the Cosmos, but God's even more than that. God is the Infinite Personhood of the Cosmos. God is not just the Infinity of Power. **God is the Infinity of Intimacy into whose arms I fall in every moment. And God/Goddess cares infinitely about every detail of my life.** And that is the intuition of Christianity. Every great religion has its unique gift. Christianity intuits the Christ moment. And Christ means that *I'm willing to die for the details of your life. I'm going to die on the cross for your sins.*

Meaning *I care infinitely and passionately. I'm with you in your pain. There is no pain in which you're alone.* So, we turn to the Infinity of Intimacy who knows our name and holds it all. And we bring before the Infinity of Intimacy our holy and our broken *Hallelujah*.

I am prayer, returned to you, God. Leonard Cohen, takes us inside to the Infinity of Intimacy, to the holy and the broken *Hallelujah.*

BARBARA MARX HUBBARD IS WITH US IN THE CONTINUITY OF CONSCIOUSNESS

We've decided to revisit some of the clips that Barbara Marx Hubbard was doing. And so, as I turn to Barbara Marx Hubbard and I turn the words to you, beloved Barbara Marx Hubbard, we're going to hear your sermon, one of the last ones you did with us, which is going to be part of resonating the code with us here.

Because Barbara Marx Hubbard, you and I talked so often about the continuity of consciousness, and we talked about what was most important too. You said something to me that was so beautiful. You said, *My heart's desire is to create the resources and the possibilities to allow you to be unimpeded in teaching the dharma in the world today.*

Then you said, *Marc, my deepest heart's desire is that after I pass we're able to go on together, to build, and that passion will be a movement in the continuity of consciousness—the continuity of consciousness we're talking about all the time.* I have text after text and email after email saying this. So, I turn my word to Barbara Marx Hubbard to resonate on this week's code.

EVOLUTIONARY LOVE CODE: TO LOVE GOD IS TO KNOW GOD

More than confessing your sins, you must confess your greatness.

Your greatness is your heart's desire.

To confess your greatness is to confess your heart's desire. To confess your heart's desire, you must know yourself, and to know yourself is to love yourself.

50

There is no knowledge without love. There is no love without knowledge.

There is no gnosis without Eros, and there is no Eros without gnosis.

Love is not merely a human experience. Love is not merely the human experience of an emotion.

Love is a perception.

Love is a perception identification complex. Love is an epistemological act which reveals ontology.

To love is to know, and to know is to love.

And yet, there is no love without knowing. There is no unknowing without love.

To love God is to know God.

To love God is to love God in the unknowing.

Part of confessing our greatness is clearly being able to confess our prayer. Because what is that prayer guiding us for? It's guiding us towards the expression of our unique greatness. And so, it's very interesting to think about what we need and what we feel we lack.

When we pray for it, we are praying as God in us that is obliging us for greatness. And I'm speaking now of being obliged for greatness right at this moment of evolution. Now, it was always true to some degree. But why is it so true today that everybody's uniqueness and unique greatness are needed? I think it's because we're at the point of evolution, the first time in human history that we've been aware of this. That we are about our turn on the spiral according to how it goes in our lifetime. Not in hundreds and hundreds of years from now, but in your life and my life—that's how it goes. It either very quickly goes down, not just to personal devolution, but to climate breakdown, to species extinction, to the seas being polluted, to the fact of our very species being threatened by our lack of expressing our unique greatness, our unique need, our unique gift, our unique genius, however you want to put it.

> *It's true that the world could go down*
> *so fast, by us, every one of us, not*
> *expressing our greatness.*

First of all, I'd like to see the importance of the Church of Evolutionary Love, the One-World Church, or the Church of Revolutionary, Infinite Creativity. I see our church arising at the tipping point of evolution.

I understand why we didn't arise earlier because people really didn't know. They put it up to God, they put it up to the emperor, or they put it up to the president. **Now that we know we cannot look to any of those "power centers," we're then forced to look at the inner power within ourselves.** We have to confess our greatness. And whose greatness is it that we're really confessing at this little tipping point for the very first time?

Now I am declaring that the Saturday church is the church of the self-organizing universe. In the church of the self-organizing universe, we call upon the self-organizing power that has taken us from quarks to consciousness, asking it to carry us the next step—to open our arms wide enough in this church to let them all in: all the deplorables, including ourselves.

Right now, our generation is the one that has to wake up collectively. When I first read Teilhard de Chardin. I noticed that evolution seems to be rising to greater consciousness, more freedom, more complexity and love, from single-cell to us.

Then I noticed that that impulse is my desire for more consciousness, more freedom, and more love. I began to realize, oh, my God, *evolution is me,* desiring this. I'm not desiring it outside of evolution. I'm desiring it *as* evolution.

If I know that I'm evolution desiring greatness, freedom, love, order, kindness, and blessing—**if I know that I'm evolution desiring this—does that empower me to desire with a passion far greater than my own individuality?**

Because I remember that when I first got hold of this one.

> My brother, Louis, who was of a totally different kind. He was in the oil business, and he thought the important thing was to go and play tennis and get as many girls as possible. So, I told him about Conscious Evolution, and I told him that I had discovered through Teilhard de Chardin that there is a pattern in the process, and that I seem to be going in the same direction as the pattern. I want consciousness, I want freedom, I want more love, and I asked him how he felt.
>
> And he looked completely stunned and said, *Do you think, are you actually saying, Barbara Marx Hubbard, that you are affecting evolution? You must be crazy.*

In other words, he couldn't see that he too was an expression of evolution. I think one of the great jumps of our lifetime at this tipping point is the discovery of evolution, discovery of the story toward greater consciousness, freedom, order, and love. And at the same time, the discovery that *you and I are that.*

When we're praying, we are, in some sense, God praying for the Godhood that God has given to every one of us.

And so, let's just go through and imagine that our generation, right now, that this church is essential to gather us together, so that we have the boldness, the presence, and the greatness, to yearn for the evolution of ourselves and our entire species through this breakdown point.

What do we see here? How in the world are we going to break through? What would be a future of greatness? What would be the future of humanity if we actually were great, if every one of us were to give our total gift?

Well, you know, there's a phrase which I've quoted many times that I happen to love: *Mine eyes have seen the glory of the coming of the Lord. He tramples on the vintage where the grapes of wrath are stored.*

It's interesting to imagine the implicit problem we're facing, the so-called death of our species. Due to the challenge of evolution itself, this means we have to be able to imagine what it would be like if everything we know we can do worked.

We have to be able to put it together, as God would put it together through us.

And so, I'll conclude by saying that I can envision a society that we are initiating—right here and now—to heal the Earth, to free people from hunger, disease and war, and to begin the vast expression of the depth of our inner space as individuals, and of our outer space as being born into a universe of billions of galaxies.

In that sense, our crisis is a birth—which is dangerous but natural—whereby we can heal our own body and the planetary Earth.

But that's the very beginning of us becoming a new species. In church we call it *Homo amor,* and I call it *Homo amor universalis.*

That is to say loving the Earth, healing the people, treating the people, and then saying, *Hello, we're being born as a universal species.*

And with that and with turning to Marc as a member of this *Homo amor* species, I turn my word to you, Marc.

OUR CLARIFIED HEART'S DESIRE BECOMES PART OF THE FIELD OF DESIRE

Now what does *my heart's desire* mean? This is so important. Desire is not ours. Heart's desire is not our desire. It's not our small desire. It's desire that we have purified. We have purified it so clearly, that our desires become part of the Field of Desire.

No one's heart's desire lives alone. Heart's desire is not our talents; it is often not what we feel good doing. **Heart's desire means that in a clarified moment in time our hearts opened. When our hearts opened, we entered to the inside, and we saw clearly.** We spoke the word, and we spoke the word in a commitment. We spoke the word to ourselves, but we spoke the word in a way that was imprinted on God's and Goddess's heart.

Then to be Outrageous Lovers is not to forget that moment. Faith is to be faithful to the memory.

It's to know that our heart's desire is not *how do I feel?*

Buddha said, "Have few desires, but have great ones." Our heart's desire can be painful to us. Once we step into our heart's desire, we are opened by it, but there might be a period of time where it's really hard. We might not even feel like following our heart's desire. Keep in mind though that the heart's desire is not a feel-good, superficial thing like, "Follow your bliss."

Heart's desire is where our desire opens up in complete clarity, aligned with the desire of the larger Field of Desire. To do that, we must purify the fundamental lack of clarity that gets in the way of our heart's desires. We can ask: *How does my desire serve the larger Field of Desire? Who does it impact? What does it uplift?* Once we open to our heart's desire, we commit to it fully—we're in, all the way.

Heart's desire is forever. It doesn't mean it doesn't change forms, but it means that when I'm in the Field of Desire, I am in service to the larger Field of Desire. Sometimes people come to me and they say, "Marc, you

know, what do you mean by saying I am evolution? It's my life, it's *my* life."
No, no, if it's your life, you're going to have a heart attack because you won't
be able to handle the outrageous pain of life.

We live in a world of outrageous pain and the only response to outrageous
pain is Outrageous Love. **Outrageous Love is not the small love. It's not
the love of romance for one person that excludes everyone else.**

Outrageous Love is the love that moves Reality. My Outrageous Act of Love
and my heart's desire is to commit Outrageous Acts of Love. Now there's
going to be a moment when I'm aroused. Parents and children, man and
woman come together, they're aroused and they create a baby. The baby
emerges from that moment of joined genes. Does everyone get that?

There's a moment of arousal. Joined genes create a baby, then you've got to
raise that baby. I've got four kids—they're awesome. Kids are the source of
the greatest joy and the greatest pain. There are lots of times over the next
20 years when I'm working with my child that doesn't feel ecstatic. But my
heart's desire was that moment of arousal when we recognized each other
and looked into each other's eyes. That was the moment that aroused heart's
desire. When heart's desires come together, they create a new moment.

Then we're committed to that moment. We're faithful to the memory.
Sometimes we open, sometimes it's gorgeous and glorious, and other times
it's hard. But when we come to the moment that Barbara came to and we
look back on our lives—we're filled with a radical joy because we remain
committed.

The only thing we're held accountable for in life:

+ Did we commit to that which was aroused by our heart's
  desire?
+ Did we nurture the children?
+ Did we raise the children?

We're not just role mates committed to those children. We're not just soul
mates looking into each other's eyes; we're whole mates. We're whole mates,

meaning that we're not just joining genes in arousal and then committed to the baby.

We're joining genius in a moment of arousal in which we know, on the Inside of the Inside, that even though God's name doesn't seem to be mentioned anywhere, we're in. Your heart's desire is everything. So, as we close, friends, I want to invite everyone to go into the chat box and just say: *I am committed to my greatness. I'm committed to my greatness and my greatness is my heart's desire.*

Barbara, we love you madly. *Mine eyes have seen the glory.*

We're going to end with: "How could anyone ever tell you that you are anything less than beautiful?"

"How Could Anyone?" — Libby Roderick [See Appendix]

CHAPTER FOUR

AWAKENING HOMO AMOR: PARTICIPATING IN THE EVOLUTION OF LOVE

Episode 134 — May 4, 2019

WELCOMING BARBARA

Good morning everyone, and we are now setting our intention. So, the first intention I want to set this week in church is Barbara Marx Hubbard. *Welcome love, it's so great to have you with us.*

Barbara Marx Hubbard, my evolutionary partner and whole mate who passed to the next world a few weeks ago. But it was not even a few weeks ago. It was three weeks ago if I'm going to be exact. It's just so shocking. And I wake up in the morning and I want to read the email—Barbara would every morning send me a long email with all of our visions and a kind of recapitulation of everything we talked about with our hopes for the day. And we would communicate four or five times in the middle of the day.

And Barbara, we are here and we are committed and you are here with us. I was just at your friend, Bill Gladstone's, the other day and we felt you there with us. So, Barbara, a big welcome.

But I feel like we did such a eulogy and the memorial service was so beautiful and so holy. It was also so sudden.

Eulogy services are memorials. It was so sudden and we're not complete. It feels like there's another step we want to just be able to express our appreciation, to share the impact, to send Barbara in her transition.

As she's now rising through worlds—in the first thirty days in the mystical traditions, we rise to the next worlds. We just want to really just presence Barbara in this moment. *And we're with you and you're with us, and we're committed. And all the resources, and all the energy, and all the love, that you poured into Evolutionary Church are valuable and good, and holy, and may it lift you higher, so, amen, amen.*

THE GLOBAL INTIMACY DISORDER: WE DON'T HAVE A SHARED STORY

Now, we're Setting Intention, we have an order of service; through the order of service we can ground ourselves. What is our intention?

Our intention is to say, each of us to ourselves and to each other: *I'm ready to play a larger game.* **I'm ready to play a larger game.** I'm ready to step out of my organization, my life, my religion, my family, all those beautiful, gorgeous things that I'm committed to—and I continue, I should continue to be committed to—*but I'm willing to take my place at the seat of history, and to realize that at this moment in history we're facing an existential threat unlike any we have faced at any other moment in history.*

The very survival of humanity is at stake:

- We realize that the gap between the haves and the have-nots is growing wider and wider.
- We realize that there are a million suicides a year in the world and probably 25 million—best estimate—of attempted suicides.
- We realize we're living in a world in which we're all physically connected, but we're non-intimate.

And the source of existential threat in all of its different modes that we've talked about, is what we call here in church: a global intimacy disorder.

The global intimacy disorder is rooted in one primary factor that's ignored in all of the policy conversations, which is that we don't have a shared story.

We don't have a shared story. And by story, we don't mean something made-up or fanciful conjecture. We mean the best information available to us from the interior and exterior sciences—from mysticism, anthropology, physics, chemistry, molecular biology, and all the great traditions—woven together in a new configuration. These parts come together in a whole greater than the sum of the parts: a new configuration of intimacy, which is a new story. **We don't have a story, so we're living—billions of people around the world—in this malaise, in this tragic absence of story.**

And so we can't find each other. We experience a global intimacy disorder and that global intimacy disorder is the source of alienation, it's the source of destruction, it's the source of suicide. And it's the source of what we might call a "Global Action Paralysis." **The Global Action Paralysis and the global action confusion are rooted in a global intimacy disorder.**

And so our intention in church is: *I want to play a larger game. I'm ready to play a larger game.* That's what we're here for. That's where we are, the Buddha; the church itself is the Buddha; the *Sangha* is the Buddha.

> We are here to stand for that larger game. I'm ready to play a larger game.

And the next sentence is:

> I'm ready to participate in the evolution of love.

That's our intention.

I'm ready to play a larger game. I'm ready to participate in the evolution of love, with you together as a band of Outrageous Lovers telling the new story and reweaving the source code.

Our intention is now set and with delight, with honor, with holy Eros falling and moving right around us and through us as Outrageous Lovers, we turn to our code.

EVOLUTIONARY LOVE CODE: YOUR DEEPEST HEART'S DESIRE IS THE SOURCE OF GREAT JOY

It's time to move from *Homo sapiens* to *Homo amor*, or what we sometimes call *Homo amor universalis*.

There's not just one Big Bang but there are four big bangs. The First Big Bang is cosmological evolution. The Second Big Bang is biological Evolution. The Third Big Bang is the awakening of the noosphere, the word created by the human heart and mind. We call this cultural evolution. The Fourth Big Bang is the awakening of evolution to itself, in us, the emergence of conscious evolution.

There's one more Big Bang. The Fifth Big Bang is the emergence of *Homo amor* or what we call *Homo amor universalis*. We call this the birth of *Homo amor*.

The first step in *Homo amor* is the move from our false self to a healthy separate self. The second step in the emergence of *Homo amor* is the emergence, or this move from True Self to Unique Self. The third step is the move from Unique Self to Evolutionary Unique Self. And the fourth step is the emergence of what we call Unique Self Symphonies.

All of this together is the emergence of *Homo amor*. Unique Self Symphony is a symphony of desire.

We realize that we do not create our desire, but our desires create us. *Have few desires but have great ones.*

Your greatest desire, your deepest heart's desire, is your confession of greatness.

Your deepest desire is not always what you want to do, or what you have fun doing, but it is the source of great joy.

And your deepest desire is what evolution needs from you.

Barbara, you're resonating with us, *Homo amor*. We're awakening *Homo amor*.

I often mention my friend and colleague, Yuval Harari. You've all read his book, *Homo Deus*. Yuval gets it. He gets that **we're in this place where artificial intelligence, machine learning, climate change, suicide, mental breakdown, the gap between haves and have-nots, and a series of six or seven other things that are threatening the very structure of who we are.**

> *We're at a phase shift in history as momentous possibly as moving from single-celled to multi-cellular life six hundred million years ago.*

And people are asleep. Everyone's playing in the same old game, and history is moving on. And we're not even going to know what hit us unless we step up to the stage of history and we feel, and we emerge—not just a new project, not a book on this, and a book on that—we emerge in our species. We go from *Homo Deus*, Yuval's vision of human beings biohacking their way to immortality—a dystopian vision of *Hunger Games* and *Blade Runner*—and we emerge as *Homo amor*.

Let's just chant for a second. There are thousands of us from all over the world. We just want to own and hold one chant, one simple chant, as we are repatterning Evolutionary Church in these weeks. And here's the chant. It goes like this: *Amor*.

It's the love that defines the Cosmos. Solomon said, *Its insides are lined with love.* **It's Evolutionary Love—the animating Eros and energy that drives and suffuses this name *Homo amor*—**which invites the new human, which invites the new humanity.

WHAT IS *HOMO AMOR?*

Homo amor is an expression of a set of ideas I've been working with in different forms for the last twenty years. But it's a particular term that I coined in response to my colleague Yuval Harari's book, *Homo Sapiens*, followed by *Homo Deus*.

Homo Sapiens and *Homo Deus* are two books that have had an enormous impact on the leading edges of Western intelligence. And they are books that are fundamentally dystopian. Yuval doesn't bring new knowledge to the table, but he brings a commanding writing presence. He brings a dystopian, disturbing vision that he's committed to putting in the forefront of culture. I think he's doing something important, but his vision, as he acknowledges, is essentially a dystopian vision of human beings biohacking their way to some limited version of immortality. **Of course, only the most wealthy, the most privileged, will be able to accomplish that biohacking, and the rest of the human beings will be, to use Yuval's phrase, *useless.***

It used to be that we were worried about our place in the world, but we thought: *Well, the elite can't actually destroy us because they need us, they need us for labor.* That's no longer going to be true. With the exponential emergence of technology, human beings won't be needed for most labor. And so, Harari's point is that *from the perspective of the wealthy elite who have bio-hacked their way to immortality, most human beings will actually be useless.*

I've written extensively, not in response to Yuval directly, but in response to the set of ideas that Yuval has brought together in one book that has been around for the last twenty years. I've talked about these three pieces.

- ◆ The first is your Unique Self.
- ◆ The second is this vision of *Homo amor*.
- ◆ And the third is what we might call Unique Self Symphony.

And *Homo amor* means something very simple.

That which drives Reality, that which animates Reality, is Eros. Eros is— and here's the definition—the experience of being radically alive, moving towards ever-deeper contact and ever-larger wholeness which yields in its wake ever more depth, creativity, and transformation. That's Eros. Eros drives Reality.

In many ways, Eros is another name for Love or Evolutionary Love. **Reality is animated by, suffused by, and driven by Evolutionary Love.** The self-organizing universe is isomorphic with—a synonym for, or precisely the same as what we mean when we say—Eros or Evolutionary Love.

The self-organizing universe organizes towards higher and higher levels of love, care, and concern for freedom, consciousness, and elegant order.

The human being is not separate from that universe. We not only live in the universe; the Universe lives in us. We're not only in evolution; evolution is in us.

I realize that I am an expression of evolution, but not just evolution, Evolutionary Love, of Eros. I'm an irreducibly unique expression of Eros and Evolutionary Love. I'm a unique expression of the LoveIntelligence and LoveBeauty, that is the initiating and animating Eros of All-That-Is, which lives in me, as me, and through me.

As such, I have an irreducibly unique gift that comes from the merger of my unique perspective and my unique quality of intimacy that are needed by All-That-Is, and I join my gift with the other unique gifts of like-minded people (in Barbara's beautiful phrase—I've joined not genes, but genius, or what Barbara and I call in our new book, *Whole Mates*) to create what I would call a Unique Self Symphony.

And our unique instrument is the unique expression of intimacy and *LoveIntelligence* that lives in us, as us, and through us. So, as such, *Homo amor* is not *homo deus*, the elite that bio hack their way to immortality, but the recognition that:

- Every human being is an irreducibly Unique Self.
- Every human being is an irreducibly unique configuration of intimacy with irreducible value, with irreducible quality, with irreducible meaning.
- And as such, each human being deserves to have their story heard, their poem read.

We have to support every human being's ability to maximize their irreducibly, uniquely gorgeous expression of *LoveIntelligence*. That's what I call *Homo amor*.

WHO IS *HOMO AMOR UNIVERSALIS*?

Now, that *Homo amor* comes together with *Homo universalis* that Barbara's been talking about beautifully for so many years. And Barbara, of course, has spoken extensively about *Homo universalis,* and far be it for me to speak for her. But, I'll just say one word about it, which I think is critical because I think it's gorgeous.

When Barbara talks about *Homo universalis* she talks about many things, but I'm just going to pick one of them which is the emergence of tech, of technological power.

The human being has always been *Homo habilis*. We've always made technology. Technology is not foreign to the human being. Ever since the first hominid picked up a stick on the savanna between 100 and 300 thousand years ago, we've used technology to overcome boundaries that separated us, to overcome limitations, and to reach for the fruit that was beyond our grasp. And we're using technology in the same way today, as we move towards a world in which, as Barbara loved to say, *The powers of Roman Gods are available to us.* **We're rewriting the script of matter, biotech, nanotech, gene splicing, the script of life itself, Artificial intelligence. We're creating a new possibility of sentience. Those are all qualities of *Homo universalis*.**

When we infuse and bring together *Homo universalis* with *Homo amor*, we create a vision of the new humanity and the new human. When two people come together and honor each other, they meet each other in Evolutionary Love. Just like evolution always creates proximity between people, it creates love, mutuality, shared vision, and something new is born—a new emergent, greater than the sum of the parts, so too...

> *Homo amor universalis is not just a vision of the future, but it actually is the process of evolution at work, incarnate before us.*

I am delighted, honored, beside myself, and ecstatic to celebrate the birth of the new human and new humanity—the birth of *Homo amor universalis* —and awaken the new species.

HOMO AMOR UNIVERSALIS: A NEW UNDERSTANDING OF ALL OUR DIMENSIONS

Thank you, Marc, and I just want to say a word of how I feel when I say *Homo amor universalis*. I can get, internally, all these parts coming together as a new whole. *Homo amor universalis* also has deep evolutionary spirituality, has a profound vocational arousal.

Everybody who is a member of it wants to be more in love and do more. It seemed to want to join genius, where people are looking for partners to be greater than they can be alone. And you add high tech to that, like you said, with powers of ancient gods combined with Evolutionary Love, evolutionary spirituality, and evolutionary vocation.

I want to say this is an awesome species, and we're all members of it. When I do meditations now, my mantra is: *I am Homo amor universalis.*

> *And what happens is that I feel new because I am able to place myself in the field of the new species, as a member of a new species.*

I just want to conclude with the blessing that this particular event of *Homo amor universalis* is coming together as the students and as the new humans. And there are microcosms of humans everywhere on Earth who are evolving.

I'd like to say a blessing that out of this new name and this new understanding of all our dimensions—that this species will arise on Earth in time to avoid the destruction we could do through climate change and species extinction. I hope we're going to create, as *Homo amor universalis*, a future equal to our love and our creativity.

Thank you, Marc, and thank you for being my partner in co-conceiving this. And we bless everybody as being members of the emerging species.

HOMO AMOR IS OUR RESPONSE TO THE SECOND SHOCK OF EXISTENCE

Thank you. *Hallelujah. Amen.* I think everyone understands why we wanted to play that recording of Barbara.

The Word is good, and the Word is moving through us—we are evangelicals.

Oh my god, don't get excited, let's be proper. Why would we get excited?

Well, of course, we're excited. This is the new story. Da Vinci is sitting in Florence. Europe has been decimated. You can't go to every village and heal individual people. There's only one thing you can do. You can tell a new story. And we are at that phase shift. We're at that moment, and we're at the leading edge of the leading evidence.

Our responsibility is that we are the band of Outrageous Lovers in Evolutionary Church taking responsibility to tell the new story. And we are declaring this day: I am *Homo amor universalis*. We're moving beyond *Homo sapiens* where we live in an egocentric, semi-narcissistic, dog-eat-dog world. No, we can't live that way. It's that impulse that's brought us to realize the second shock of existence. The first shock was the realization of death. Human beings die, and we responded with all of religion and all of culture. The God-voice spoke.

Now we're at the second shock of existence, which is not the death of the individual human, but it's the potential death of humanity. And so, we need a new God-voice. We need to move from *Homo sapiens* to *Homo amor,* and so we're declaring on this day that **the word is good**.

THE INNER EXPERIENCE OF *HOMO AMOR UNIVERSALIS* IS THAT REALITY IS LITERALLY 50/50

This is beyond *my schedule and your schedule.* This is beyond *starting a local organization.* We are starting the church of Evolutionary Love. Feel it in yourself. Can you feel that in yourself? Can you feel it?

Actually feel yourself transfiguring. This is what Christ's path meant when they talked about transfiguration. We've all gone through great suffering. Is there anyone in this church who hasn't gone through some form of crucifixion, and some form of breaking, and some form of shattering?

Well now it's time for resurrection, but we resurrect as *Homo amor universalis.* And the way you feel it is: oh, my God, all of history depends on me. My next action tips the balance.

The inner experience of Homo amor universalis is that Reality is literally 50/50.

Can you feel that, everyone? It's 50/50, and **my very next action is going to tip the scale.** I act not just for myself and not just for my family, as beautiful as that is. And not just for my country, as gorgeous as that is. Not just egocentric, not just ethnocentric, not even just worldcentric for every human being.

I act for the Cosmos; I have cosmocentric intimacy.

I am evolution. Every animal, every plant, and every quark—it's all in me.

And it really is all in me. The deepest information of the new sciences says: *not only do we live in an Intimate Universe, but the Intimate Universe lives in me.*

When we say, *I am God,* it's not New Age nonsense. It's not a kind of narcissistic grab. It all lives in me. God holds me, God lives in me, and so my very next act tips the balance. I act for the sake of evolution and as *Homo amor universalis.*

And here's our practice. I ask one question and one question only: What does evolution need from me in the next moment? That's the only question you ever need to ask. Now, it might be starting a soup kitchen, and it might be taking care of your son. And it might be being a great son to your mom. And it might be calling your brother in Wisconsin. **But we're doing it for the sake of evolution.** And so I take care of my immediate, I take care of myself.

I love myself open. I love my close, intimate circle open, and then I go the next step.

WHAT DOES EVOLUTION NEED FROM ME IN THIS NEXT MOMENT?

When I can feel that living and moving inside of me then we are birthing the consciousness of *Homo amor.*

Can you imagine that, friends? Can you imagine seven billion people rising on the planet in a self-organizing universe, bringing all of our holy and broken *Hallelujah* before the Divine who knows our name and then partnering with God and saying: I am *Homo amor universalis,* and I have one question: *What does evolution need from me in the next moment?*

Here's the crazy story. The crazy story is: *that is my heart's desire.*

My heart's desire is to align with evolution. And that's where my joy is. It's not always fun, but it's always joyful. And then it gets crazy fun because it goes from joy to the deepest delight you can possibly imagine. See, when you're in your life, even when it's hard, it's filled with joy.

What does evolution need from me in the next moment? That is my heart's desire. Wow!

CHAPTER FIVE

A CRISIS OF TOUCH: BECOMING THE MOTHER TO EACH OTHER

Episode 135 — May 11, 2019

GOD IN FIRST PERSON, SECOND PERSON, AND THIRD PERSON

Welcome, everyone, to the Evolutionary Church. It is a delight and a pleasure to be here. Yesterday, I was just communing and meditating with beloved Barbara, who founded the church with us, and we prepared a beautiful church for today. We're going to be up-levelling and taking huge next steps forward in the coming weeks. Let's open with a beautiful and gentle chant to find our way.

In church, one of the things that's unbelievably important is reclaiming God because we're afraid to talk about God. One of our principles in church is: the god you don't believe in doesn't exist. But who is God? We always talk about these three faces in church, the new Holy Trinity of Evolutionary Church. As we move towards renaming our church, which Barbara and I were talking about right before she passed, as the One Church. It's a church, it's a synagogue, it's a mosque, it's a secular humanist center—we're the One-World Church.

When we speak to God, we speak to the God who lives in us—God in the first-person, *tat tvam asi*,[7] *Thou Art That*. God is running and moving through me.

We speak to God who is the laws of physics, the laws of chemistry, and molecular biology, billions and billions of light years of the universe, and amazing complexity beyond imagination. **All the supercomputers of Reality couldn't manifest that ceaselessly creative Cosmos. That's God in the third-person. That's the incessant creativity of Cosmos.**

God in the first-person is God having a "me" experience. This is a fundamental category of the ancient mystics in the *Zohar*: God is *Ani*: I. God is *Hu*: It, third person. But God is also *Ata*: You. God is the Mother, the Lover, the Beloved; **God is all three.**

If you understand what's happened, this is the deepest *dharma* we can start church with. Different sectors of society are fighting with each other, arguing over which God is the right God. For example, all of the Eastern mystical world, all of the ashrams—that entire, beautiful world of enlightenment which I've taught in and have been a part of for many years—say: *Well, the only real God is the God that lives in you. The God of the churches and the synagogues are not real. The God of the academy—that's not real. Only God in first person.* The ashram kind of mocks the academy.

Now, the academy of science says: *No, it's not God in first person. God who lives in you, we don't even know what that is.* Carl Sagan, for example, said that *the Cosmos is God in third person.*

Often, *God in third person people* don't even identify and use the word god. They talk about the creativity of Cosmos. Stuart Kauffman, in his wonderful book *The Sacred Universe*, talks about the incessant, ceaseless creativity of cosmos—a phrase that I'm slightly adapting, changing, and transmuting.

---

7 One of the *Mahāvākyas* or *great sayings* from the *Upanishads*, central texts of Vedantic philosophy in Hinduism.

Those are the *third-person people*. Let's call them the scientists and the academy—they have nothing to do with the *ashram*,[8] and the *ashram* has nothing to do with the academy. Both of them deny the church, the synagogue, and the mosque which say that *it's God in second person*.

This is our Evolutionary Love Code: God in second person, which is God who knows me. Like Rumi, who falls into the arms of the Beloved.

- God who knows my name.
- God who speaks to me.
- God in whose arms I fall; wherever I fall, I fall into Her arms.
- That God can be the Mother.
- That God can be the Lover and the Beloved of the Song of Solomon.
- But it's God in second person, how gorgeous!

Let's open today with God in second person; I'm going to do a chant with you for God in the second person, God who's the Infinity of Intimacy, who knows our name.

Barbara is going to help me chant, and we're going to do a *God in second person chant*, and we're going to particularly pick the face of God who is the face of the Mother.

Welcome from all over the world. Ten thousand of us have signed up for Evolutionary Church, the One Church, to begin the Outrageous Love revolution.

ALL THE RIVERS FLOW BACK TO THE SEA

The image is, as it's called in the text of Psalms, *nahar yotzei me'eden*, a river that flows from Eden. *Kol hanekhalim holkhim el-hayam*,[9] the Bible says, *all*

---

8 A spiritual hermitage or monastery, traditionally found in India and other parts of South Asia. It serves as a place of retreat, learning, and spiritual practice, often under the guidance of a guru or teacher.

9 Ecclesiastes 1:7.

the rivers flow back to the sea. The sea is the ocean, the Mother, the Lover, the Beloved. Why? Have you ever walked by the ocean and just looked at the ocean? She's so beautiful. You look at her just for her own sake. She's tumultuous, and she can swallow us up. She can feed us, nourish us, and bathe us.

So, the Goddess, She, the Mother, the Lover, is always the ocean.

Here's the chant, "The River is Flowing":[10]

> *The river is flowing,*
> *Flowing and growing,*
> *The river is flowing*
> *Back to the sea.*
> *Mother, carry me*
> *A child I will always be,*
> *Mother, carry me*
> *Back to the sea.*

Amen! Happy Mother's Day to every mother.

The mother is every mother in the world, but it's also the mother we didn't have.

It might be our mother or father; any one of us might be the Mother.

Mother is the quality that sees us and knows us at our best, that holds us whenever we fall, and that stands for us, even when we don't know how to stand for ourselves. And we can bring everything to the Mother; we bring our deepest prayer to the Mother.

---

10 Gila Antara, "The River Is Flowing," *Lieder zwischen Himmel und Erde* (Antara Music, 1998).

THE SACRED TECHNOLOGY OF CHANT

When we chant, we're opening up because chant is a key to the inner door of the Cosmos. Chant actually opens up the Inside of the Inside. The chant takes us to the interior face of the Cosmos, to what, in the Hebrew tradition, is called the Holy of Holies.

Remember the *Raiders of the Lost Ark*, Indiana Jones? The Lost Ark is the Ark of the Covenant, and the Ark is in what's called the Holy of Holies. The other name for the Holy of Holies is: *the Inside of the Inside*.

How did the High Priests get into the Holy of Holies? Through chant! The Levites chanted in the Temple, and the Aborigines chanted The One Song in the Outback of Australia, and the great American Indians do their chants, and the Catholics. Yes, there's holiness, there's sparks of holiness in the originating impulse of the Catholic Church, although it's lost a lot of its originality. In the synagogue, the mosque, the Taoist center, the Buddhist center, and the Kashmir Shaivite temple, there is chant.

Chant is a sacred technology, but it's not a song—it's not a Girl Scout song. I often want to chant just for 10 hours at a time. You slowly open the Inside of the Inside; it's a door that opens it. That's why it feels good, because you're feeling the very goodness of Cosmos. The great Solomon writes, *tocho ratzuf ahava, Its insides are lined with love*, and the way I get to the inside is chant. Chant is the mathematics and music of intimacy.

EVOLUTIONARY LOVE CODE: EVOLUTION IS THE EVOLUTION OF INTIMACY

> We live in an Intimate Universe, and the Intimate Universe
> lives in us, and evolution is the evolution of intimacy.

This is our code today that we're going to talk about. *We live in an Intimate Universe, and the Intimate Universe lives in us, and evolution is the evolution of intimacy.* There are two paths to find our way into the inside of the Intimate Universe.

One path into the inside of Intimate Universe, believe it or not, is mathematics. The second way into the inside of the Intimate Universe is chant, through music. The two faces of the Intimate Universe are mathematics and music.

Do you remember Pythagoras? Pythagoras was that great pre-Socratic philosopher who studied music and mathematics, and he serves as a perfect example of one who truly understands—one who grasped that music and math are two faces of The One.

Physics finds mathematics as the way into the Inside of the Inside. Complexity theory—which is one of the most important developments in science—is the mathematics of intimacy. **Music and mathematics, which are two faces of The One, are the intimate Cosmos revealed.** When we chant, we're opening a door to the Inside of the Inside.

Barbara is going to be here with us today. We're going to play a video from Barbara, and I'm going to share with you what Barbara shared as well. Barbara Marx Hubbard, my profound evolutionary partner who passed to the next world a few weeks ago, but who's deeply with us in church in these weeks.

All over the world in this moment, we're going to chant this together. Again, we're chanting as practice. We're accessing the interior face of the Cosmos, the Inside of the Inside. It's such an honor to be here in The One Church, which is the revolution; **this is the Outrageous Love revolution.**

Are you ready to tell the new story?

OUR INTENTION IS TO TELL THE NEW STORY

Here's our intention in church. It's always a two-line intention which we set at the beginning of church, and it's so beautiful to be here.

Here's the question we ask ourselves: *Are you ready to play a larger game? Are we for real?*

78

Or are we making this up? Are we going through the motions? Or are we awake and alive? Are we enthusiastic?

Am I getting enthusiastic? I am—because I'm feeling the gorgeousness of being here. Enthusiasm means we're *enthused* with spirit.

We are afraid to be enthusiastic. We're afraid to be evangelical. We're Evolutionary Love evangelicals together.

Are we ready to play a larger game?

Here's the second question: *Are you ready to participate in the evolution of love?*

So, are you ready? Are we ready to be evangelicals of the Good News, which is the new story?

The new story is the only response to existential risk that can actually work. Our intention in church aligns with what da Vinci told us during the Renaissance: there is no way to heal the Black Death or any plague through conventional means. The only thing we can do, said Leonardo da Vinci—who is a co-founder with us of the Evolutionary Church, along with Leonard Cohen—is to tell a new story and weave the parts together into a larger intimacy.

To tell that new story is to participate in the evolution of love. Because what is a new intimacy? A new intimacy is *parts that are woven together to form a whole greater than the sum of the parts.* That's the new intimacy.

The new story that responds to existential risk is the highest story there is. It's the best story there is. **It's only a new story that can bring us together— that can let us understand that that which unites us is so much greater than that which divides us.**

Every challenge we face is a global challenge. We have to have a global shared story, the *One Church* story.

THE ONE CHURCH IS THE SHARED MUSIC OF ALL THE GREAT RELIGIONS

Now remember, The One Church doesn't obliterate or eliminate Mormonism, Judaism, Catholicism, Lutheranism, or other forms of Christianity, Sufism, or Taoism. In other words, all the individual religions are the unique selves of different faces of Spirit. Here's the *dharma: Every religion is a Unique Self; it's a unique expression of Spirit. Then the religions come together, and they play the larger music.*

The One Church is the shared music of all the great religions.

- ◆ It's the shared principles of goodness, truth, and beauty.
- ◆ It's the shared story that's greater than all that divides us.
- ◆ It's that shared story that's going to take us home.

We are being this church together. The next Buddha is the *Sangha*. We are the *Sangha*. We are the community.

By the way, if anything I say annoys you, forget about me. Forgive me; I'm wrong.

- ◆ We're just channeling it through together.
- ◆ We are the One Church.
- ◆ We are evolving the source code.
- ◆ We're writing the new Evolutionary Love Codes.
- ◆ We are the new Renaissance.

It's hard to believe that; you think it's happening someplace else, but it's not. There are all sorts of great efforts in the world, but they're not writing the new story. **It's only the new story that can take us home.**

Weaving the new story from the best of physics, chemistry, anthropology, and the best of all the disciplines into a larger one—that Renaissance move is what takes us from dystopia to utopia. Barbara and I founded the church on that principle, and now the church is all of ours. It's articulating and evolving that new story.

Part of that new story is that God is actually back in the game. We can't read God out of the game. We can't reduce God to some expression of our own narcissistic fantasy. It can't be *god owned by one religion who's a cosmic vending machine.*

- God lives in us: the first face of God.
- God is the incessant creativity of Cosmos: the third face of God.
- But God also holds us in this moment. God both speaks through us and is holding us. Feel Her holding us.

That's what the Christ moment was about. She's holding us in every moment. She loves us so madly that She died for us, and She's reborn for us. There's no religion that's not holding some core truth. The Christ moment, the Sufi moment is, as Rumi says: *I'm falling into the arms of the Beloved; I fall into the arms of the Mother.* Let's chant now from that place.

CRISIS IN THE WORLD: WE'VE FORGOTTEN WHAT IT MEANS TO TOUCH EACH OTHER

> We live in an Intimate Universe, and the Intimate Universe lives in us, and evolution is the evolution of intimacy.

We're going into our code this week, the code of radical intimacy, the code of mutually touching each other in the deepest way in the world. That's our code for Mother's Day this week and our Evolutionary Love Code.

Our code this week is about what I want to call a "crisis of touch." *MeToo* is a crisis of touch, where we don't know how to touch each other, we're afraid to touch each other, or we touch each other inappropriately. But we touch each other inappropriately because we don't understand what it means to touch each other. I want to talk this week in our Mother's Day sermon about a crisis of touch.

Ashley Montagu wrote a great book about the deep desire we have to be touched. What does it mean that we have a desire to be touched? First, **we**

81

have a desire to be touched emotionally. Remember Ma-Bell: *Reach out and touch someone.*

We have a desire to be touched emotionally. We want to touch each other spiritually. We want to touch each other psychologically. We want to touch each other existentially. We want to touch each other intellectually. We want to touch each other aesthetically.

We want to touch each other. Remember the caste system in India? What's the worst thing in the world you can be? **The worst thing in the world you can be is an *untouchable*,** which means you don't deserve to be touched. There's a crisis of touch in the world; we've forgotten what it means to touch each other.

And, I want to add, we're touching each other emotionally and physically, and we're always touching each other mutually; we're always touching each other with permission, and we're always touching each other with invitation.

Once we're touching each other emotionally, existentially, psychologically, artistically, intellectually, aesthetically, and spiritually, then we want to touch each other physically.

Now, to touch each other physically means we want to hug each other or shake hands. In other words, we've exiled touch—we've exiled touch to just one kind of touch, which is human sexual touch. We're going to talk about human sexual touch as well, but first, we have to reclaim touch. I want to go even deeper with you. But first, we have to reclaim touch. I want to go even deeper with you.

Let's just start with the crisis of touch. *We want to reach out and touch someone*: Ma-Bell. We want to touch each other on every level. How do we want to touch each other? Let's make a list.

- We want to touch each other spiritually.
- We want to touch each other emotionally.
- We want to touch each other artistically.

- We want to touch each other heart to heart.
- We want to touch each other musically.
- We want to touch each other intellectually, the power of ideas.
- We want to touch each other existentially.
- Finally, we want to touch each other physically.

THE ALLUREMENT TO TOUCH EACH OTHER IS FUNDAMENTAL TO COSMOS

Now let's go to the next step. Alfred North Whitehead, the great philosopher of science, talked about prehension—an idea that reflects a truth of exterior science, meaning the new sciences of quantum reality and electromagnetic attraction.

Prehension is what I want to call proto-touch. It's the desire of subatomic particles to touch each other. That's wild!

All the desires to touch each other that we just listed, **those desires live at the very molecular level of Cosmos**. Actually, in the first nanoseconds after the Big Bang, there's this desire, this allurement to touch.

The allurement to touch each other is fundamental to Cosmos. It's that which allows for the creation of matter itself. The heart of the matter is touch. There's this radical desire for mutual touching, which brings Reality into existence.

There's no greater tragedy than a subatomic particle being untouchable, like the caste system in India in which there are untouchables. But you know what we're doing in the world today? Our crisis of touch is rooted in a false metaphysics. It's the false story of separate self.

There's a false metaphysics of separate self. If I believe that I'm just a separate self, that's my metaphysics: *I am a separate, discrete monad.* If I'm separate from all that is, then I don't want you to touch me. Then any way that you touch me—emotionally, spiritually, intellectually, artistically, existentially, psychologically, physically... you hug me—that's a violation because you're violating my space.

The false metaphysics of separate self is the source of our crisis itself.

We have to understand that I'm not a separate self; we are all part of the seamless coat of the universe. But the seamless coat of the universe is not featureless; we are its unique features. We are molecules, we are atoms, we are cells, we are organisms, and we desire to touch each other.

Now you say to me, *Marc, ideas want to touch each other, that's a very nice mythopoetic image. But it's not more than a mythopoetic image, Marc. Get real!*

But stay with me. **What's an idea? An idea is a configuration of energy.** An idea means I talk about an idea, and I put that idea which is energy, which is Eros, into words. An idea is a configuration of Eros formulated in language. That's what an idea is.

Democracy is a word. But democracy is a formulation of energy that is about human freedom and human choice. It's that formulation of energy put into a word. The word is magic. The reason a word is magic is not because it's anti-science; rather—it's interior science. A word holds the Eros and energy of an idea.

For example, **abracadabra in Aramaic, *avra kehdabra*, means: *I create with my word*. That's gorgeous, because a word is a configuration of Eros.**

Now that means that words, which are configurations of Eros, yearn for each other. They want to meet each other; they want to find each other. That's what Matt Ridley, who wrote a book called *The Rational Optimist*, thought he was just talking poetically, but it's real. It's ontology. It's what he called "idea sex," meaning that ideas are allured to each other, that ideas want to touch each other.

When ideas touch each other, they come together and weave together in a new configuration of intimacy—that touching is a new story.

It gets even more gorgeous!

THE FOUR-FOLD EXILE OF TOUCH

Look what we've done. We've exiled touch. We're going to talk about the four exiles of touch. What's the first exile of touch? We've exiled touch to the human realm; we've made touch a human activity. That's not true. **Touch is the core structure of Cosmos.**

Cosmos is Reality reaching out on all levels: chemical compounds, molecular compounds, atomic structures, and amino acids. **Reality yearns to touch, and when Reality touches, new configurations and new wholes are created.** That is what Eros means.

> But what we've done is we've taken touch and exiled it to the human realm, which is exile one.
>
> Two, we've exiled touch to the realm of romantic love.
>
> Three, we've exiled touch and romantic love to one particular realm, to the sexual.
>
> Four, we've made successful sexual touching look a particular way. It's a particular form of heterosexual penetration which results in a particular kind of feeling: an explosion, generally termed orgasm, that is successful human sexual touching. We've exiled touch *horrifically.*

Now that can be, in gorgeous mutuality, one beautiful expression of touching.

That touching, and that Eros, is actually happening all the time.

We *want to* touch each other on every level and in every way, and we *want* our physical touch to be an expression of all the touching that's happening.

We also *want* to have physical touch that's not sexual touch. A third-grade teacher is not allowed to hug his student; that's tragic.

There's documentation today about fourth and fifth graders who can also be nasty and cruel—they're also not yet liberated—making false complaints against teachers who hug them.

In our generation, we're standing correctly against inappropriate touch.

I want to stand right now, in this moment with anyone here, and anyone in the world, who was violated and touched inappropriately sexually in the wrong way. In this generation, we're standing against that, and we're standing for the utter **inviolable boundaries of every person.**

Because touch that's sexual can only be *mutual* and *beautiful* and *holy*— touch between adults. That's what we stand for at this moment.

We've evolved culture, love, and consciousness. It's evolved since I was a kid. We understand this in a deeper way than we ever did. That's a given in our space.

But now that that's a given—let's go the next step. Let's touch each other non-sexually, but let's touch each other erotically.

I want to hug every single person, anyone who is willing to receive my hug, and I want to ask you to hug me. **Let's be Outrageous Lovers. Let's hug each other. Let's embrace each other. Let's embrace each other warmly.**

What does it mean to live in a world in which we're actually creating a world where we're all part of the caste of the untouchables?

What does it mean that we're all the untouchables? Oh my God, we're all untouchables!

When we create a world in which we're all untouchables, then touch pathologizes—it goes underground, and then it erupts in inappropriate touch.

- ◆ It erupts in bad pornography.
- ◆ It erupts in the MeToo crisis.
- ◆ It erupts in a world in which there's no context for touch.

Let's touch each other. You know what the Mother does? The Mother touches us. It's why we yearn for the Mother, because we trust Her touch. We trust that She's going to embrace us and hold us. We trust that we can fall into Her arms.

We all have to be the Mother to each other. **We have to hug each other, not just with our bodies, but we have to hug each other with our minds.**

WE HAVE TO HEAL THE HUG

Chibuk is the "great divine hug." If I hug too closely, it's a strangulation. If I hug too loosely, then I'm not held. **We want to be held in the arms of the Mother.** We want to touch each other in every possible way.

What does it mean if we can't hug each other?

Oh my God, crisis of touch! We're healing it right now!

We turn to Mother, who's with us, and She's holding us in every second.

CHAPTER SIX

RECLAIMING AND EVOLVING INTIMACY: EVERYONE'S IN THE CIRCLE

Episode 136 — May 18, 2019

I AM READY TO PLAY A LARGER GAME, TO PARTICIPATE IN THE EVOLUTION OF LOVE

What's our intention, friends? Our intention is, and here's the question: *Are you ready to play a larger game?* That's our question.

We cannot rely on the *Yes* of yesterday. We cannot rely on the *Yes* of last week. It's a *Yes* right now.

It's our *Yes* that resonates the Cosmos. It's our *Yes* that takes us to the next step.

The second question is: *Are we ready to participate in the evolution of love?*

Are we ready to awaken as evolution? Are we ready to awaken as the leading edge of evolution, taking responsibility for the whole story? Because whose responsibility could it be?

Where were you when the Big Bang was happening? Could you have been any place other than right there?

Reality is not a fact; Reality is a story. Reality is not an ordinary story. **Reality is a love story.** It's a love story that includes the agony and the ecstasy.

Who am I? What is my identity? I am chapter and verse in the Universe: A Love Story. My personal love story is implicated in the Universe: A Love Story.

So, I say:

- I am ready to play a larger game.
- I'm not just a narrow, separate self. I'm not just concerned with my own particular narrow version of success.
- I succeed as we succeed, and we succeed together.
- My love story is personally implicated in the Evolutionary Love Story; they are not separate.
- Who am I? I am the leading edge of evolution.

We are the leading edge of evolution together as we awaken as the next stage of evolutionary intimacy, which is the Unique Self Symphony: loving each other madly, a band of Outrageous Lovers.

We are coding and re-coding Reality. We are re-coding Reality, we are evolving the source code with the Evolutionary Love Codes.

What a delight and an honor to be here with every single person here in Evolutionary Church.

We are the leading edge of evolution.

HOMO AMOR REUNITES LOVE AND KNOWLEDGE

Our welcome chant is *Amor* as in *Homo amor*, as in the response and the next step beyond *Homo sapiens sapiens*. *Amor* is the love that lines Cosmos. I want you to just feel this with me if you can.

We had an allergic reaction in modernity against love.

This is because Christianity—in its shadows, as did other religions—hijacked love. Christian love sadly became the rationalization for the Inquisition. Islamic versions of love became the rationalizations for declaring anyone out of Islam an infidel. Love got hijacked.

We woke up to love, but love was refracted through the prism of ethnocentric consciousness. It meant *I love my people, but I kill the rest of the world.* We had this allergic reaction to love, and so we left love out of the story. **We split love and knowledge, and love became this kind of arbitrary feeling.** Love became the way you romantically fall in love at the first stage of human relationship and got exiled from the Cosmos. So, love became not Eros but pseudo-eros.

We used love to cover up our failure of Eros and our failure of storyline. The universe lost its storyline.

- We couldn't find the plotline.
- We couldn't find the thread which carried our lives through.
- We couldn't locate ourselves in a larger Universe Story, and our narratives of identity collapsed.

All we had was a kind of sappy romantic love left as a form of pseudo-eros to replace the failure of genuine Eros. Love and knowledge split.

Love became the sappy, desiccated, superficial version of romantic love, exiled to the human experience of infatuation.

Beautiful as it is, it's a big exile of love, so it collapsed—while knowledge became a particular kind of exterior scientific knowledge, which was measured only in exterior forms through the MRI, through the microscope, through the Hubble telescope. Love and knowledge got split from each other.

Homo amor reunites love and knowledge; it brings love and knowledge back together. We begin to understand:

Love itself is what produces knowledge.

If I don't love you, I can't know you. To say *I love you* is to say *I know you*. That's *Amor*, when love and knowledge come back together. **We don't just meditate our way to enlightenment; we love our way to enlightenment.**

Why? Because love generates knowledge. Enlightenment is knowledge; it's knowledge about the true nature of things. Eros and gnosis, *Amor* and knowledge, are reunited. That's *Homo amor*.

- Love is knowledge.
- Love becomes the way we find our knowledge.
- Eros becomes the way to gnosis.

That's why we're a band of Outrageous Lovers. It's not that we're bypassing knowledge. But we know that love opens up the interior face of Cosmos, which as Solomon wrote, *tocho ratzuf ahava: Its insides are lined with love.* We reinvest the scientific enterprise—the interior sciences and exterior sciences—with a wild, passionate love that opens us up to the truest knowledge that ever was. That's *Amor*.

WE PRAY TO THE INTIMATE FACE OF THE EVOLUTIONARY IMPULSE

Now we offer up prayer, and we pray to God who is not just the evolutionary impulse, but the intimate face of the evolutionary impulse. So, we come together and we offer our holy and our broken *Hallelujah*. What do we ask for? We turn to the God who is the Infinity of Intimacy, not only the Infinity of Power, and we ask for everything. We say *I pray for*, and we ask for all of our personal needs because prayer affirms the dignity of personal need. As we are now in this eleventh hour to cross this place between dystopia and utopia, we have to do it together with God. Let's pray.

AVENGERS ENDGAME: WE ALL HAVE A UNIQUE SELF SUPERPOWER

Our crisis is a birth, personally and collectively. And crisis is an evolutionary driver. Every crisis is, at its root, a crisis of intimacy.

Why is that true? This takes us an entire next step. This takes us into the Universe: A Love Story. What does the Universe: A Love Story mean?

What's the biggest movie showing all over the world right now, a record-breaking box office hit? *Avengers: Endgame*. And what's *Avengers: Endgame* about? It's about one thing, when you look at it really deeply. It's these people, this family of Avengers, who each have their individual lives, who are standing for humanity. These are Unique Selves. These are people with their superpowers.

- There's not one person on this call who doesn't have superpowers.
- There's not one person on this call who, if they're awake as an Outrageous Lover, doesn't realize that *your superpowers are needed by All-That-Is.*

But what are the Avengers fighting for? They're fighting for intimacy; they're fighting for personal intimacies. The subplots that run through the entire story are this heroic stand for humanity against the calculations of algorithms: the calculations of *how do we balance the world and how do we winnow the population.* Thanos is the algorithm of artificial intelligence, setting Reality right according to the algorithmic demands. The Avengers are human beings standing against algorithms. They're human beings standing against the calculations that are going to "solve" the problems.

These human beings are always standing for one thing. You look at Tony Stark, who's looking into his daughter's eyes, and he's looking into his wife's eyes. You look at Hawkeye, who's madly in love with that one woman in his family. You look at Captain America, who at the end of the movie, when he's warped through time, decides to leave his hero role to others, so he can spend 60 or 70 years and grow old with the beloved of his life. The entire movie is about heroism, standing for one thing: for intimacy.

But the *Avengers: Endgame* movie got intimacy just on one level—it got intimacy on the human level.

What we understand is that:

Intimacy on the human level aligns with Reality. Reality is the evolutionary story itself.

EVOLUTIONARY LOVE CODE: BIRTHING NEW STRUCTURES OF INTIMACY

Our crisis is a birth personally and collectively because crisis is an evolutionary driver. Every great crisis at its root is a crisis of intimacy.

Crisis means that someone or something is being left out of our circle.

Enlightenment means intimacy with all people and all things. Enlightenment means that there are no externalities. Evolution is the progressive deepening of intimacies; evolution is the evolution of intimacy.

Therefore:

- Every crisis in evolution at its core is a crisis in relationship; it's a crisis of intimacy.

- ◆ The way to respond to the crisis is to evolve a new level of intimacy.

We can't just restore the intimacies of yesterday, we have to evolve new structures of intimacy.

WE UNLEASH NEW SYNERGIES IN THE WORLD

We're a Unique Self Symphony here, where unique intimacies come together and form a larger WeSpace. We unleash new synergies in the world.

To awaken with my new identity as an Outrageous Lover—who has a particular intimacy to contribute to Reality, that no one else that ever was, is, or will be can contribute.

To understand that what's happening in the world today is a global intimacy disorder. There's a global intimacy disorder happening in a deep and wild way in the world. There's a global intimacy disorder, and to heal the global intimacy disorder, we need to evolve the source code; we need to restore intimacy. **Evolution is the evolution of intimacy.**

Crisis means that someone or something is being left out of the circle. There's a failure of intimacy. And enlightenment is to reclaim intimacy.

Enlightenment means intimacy with all things. Enlightenment means there are no externalities.

This is the new code. We need this church to actually speak these codes. To know that love is not a victory march, it's a cold and it's a broken *Hallelujah*.

Maybe there's a God above.

As for me, all I've ever learned from love

is how to shoot somebody who outdrew you.

What Leonard Cohen is saying is that the trite love way in which my love is separated from the rest of Reality—that doesn't work. It's *Hallelujah.*

Hallelujah means that there are no externalities in all of Reality that is singing *Hallelujah*, that is singing praise, and that is reaching for more intimacy. And my intimate story is worth living and dying for. It's worth all of us living and dying for each other's intimate stories. **When we come together and love each other madly, then we get the One Love, and we live in the One Love.**

This church, whose intention is the evolution of love, is standing for that One Love.

We need to have this church, which is like the Gospel church of the Civil Rights Movement, without which there would not have been civil rights in America. Civil rights can easily be reversed, and there's a judicial agenda to reverse many of the essential civil rights in this country. So, for this country and around the world, we need Evolutionary Love. We need a church of Evolutionary Love. We need a Gospel of Evolutionary Love. We need to be a band of Outrageous Lovers, *together.*

AVENGERS ENDGAME: I'M NOT SEPARATE FROM THE LARGER WHOLE

That Avengers movie that swept box office records all over the world had two themes. One is: love matters; personal intimacies matter. It's worth saving the world for the sake of anyone's individual, personal love. Now we're adding to that *dharma* that every individual love story is not separate or alone but is implicated in the Universe: A Love Story. It's love, all the way up and all the way down. Molecules come together intimately and form larger wholes and new intimacies.

Every crisis is a crisis of intimacy, and the crisis of intimacy is *somebody is left out of the circle.*

96

Because we don't have genuine Eros, we put someone out of the circle in order to give us an illusion that we are in the circle.

What was the other major theme of that *Avengers: Endgame* movie? The other major theme is that *death is not real.*

There's this kind of race against death, which is on one hand holy—we want to remove unnecessary death, and we want to remove all unnecessary suffering. But, at some point in the natural course of the universe, people die. But when death happens, when Tony Stark dies at the end of the movie, and he gives his life for the sake of the larger value and the larger whole, he's realizing an enlightenment moment.

The enlightenment moment is: *I'm not separate from the larger whole*, and *my value is part of the larger constellation of value.* One of the sacred axioms of Reality, which we derive and know in our own hearts, is that **if I live for myself, I'm already dead**.

I never live for myself and myself alone. I am part of Earth, and I emerge from Earth. But Earth is not the ground. Earth and blood are not the ground. No, underneath Earth and blood is consciousness, and the interior of consciousness is Outrageous Love. We're grounded not in Earth; that's a *Gaia* myth. We're grounded—and Earth itself is Outrageous Love.

That's why, as we frame our prayers here, we are grounded in Outrageous Love. Outrageous Love is the very stuff of Reality.

When Tony Stark passes… when Barbara Marx Hubbard passes, she doesn't pass from existence. She passes from our ability to access her instantly and physically hear her voice. But even that's no longer true. We just heard you, Barbara. I said six months ago, *there's going to come a day when I wish Barbara would be calling me to drive me crazy.* Barbara, where are you, beloved? I take for granted now that Barbara's calling is not going to be there, and that breaks my heart.

Barbara is with us. Barbara knows exactly what we're saying in this church, and Barbara is watching this church right now. We're grounded in Outrageous Love.

I made a promise to Barbara, and Barbara made a promise to me that we're going to ground this church in Reality. That it will become the revolutionary Evolutionary Church carrying the new story that we've committed our lives to, that's so desperately needed because we will not make it across the eleventh hour without the new story.

Friends, it's up to you. Let's be significant and step up.

- Contribute your voice.
- Contribute your prayer.
- Contribute your presence.
- Contribute your resources.

And create a vision that can literally change the future source code of Reality. This is our moment. We have a seat at the table. We are grounded.

What are we grounded in? We are grounded in Reality.

What is Reality? Reality is Outrageous Love.

Underneath the Earth, before there was any Gaia, there was Outrageous Love.

We live in a world of outrageous pain. That's true, but we *can respond* to outrageous pain. The only response to outrageous pain is Outrageous Love, and we are the band of Outrageous Lovers.

Barbara, you are with us, and we are going to stand for the evolution of love.

Are you ready to play a larger game? We are! We're ready to participate in the evolution of love.

Oh, my God! How deep is your love? I want you to breathe me. Let me be your air.

CHAPTER SEVEN

OUR TOUCH QUIVERS REALITY TO NEW IDENTITY—GOD ASKS EVERYTHING OF ME

Episode 137 — May 25, 2019

LIVING MY LIFE TO THE FULLEST, CHAPTER AND VERSE IN THE UNIVERSE: A LOVE STORY

This is our intention, which we always set at the beginning of the church. We ask ourselves a question: *Are you ready to play a larger game? Are you ready to participate in the evolution of love?* We actually realize that our life, your life, my life is an Outrageous Love Story. That your life and my life are chapter and verse in the Universe: A Love Story.

We realize, as we set our intention, that this is not quite a Harlequin romance. This is not sweet and saccharine. As Rudolf Otto, the great German theologian, wrote: *It's not all sweetness and light.*

In this love story, there's agony and ecstasy. **But it's all part of the love story, and we can bear with the agony and transform it into ecstasy when we know it's not meaningless.** Dostoevsky said: *I can deal with any circumstance if I know the why—if I know the context.*

The context of my life is: my life is an Outrageous Love Story.

When I live my life to the fullest, my full being and full becoming, **when I crystallize my unique risk, take my unique risk, and commit my Outrageous Acts of Love—I participate and step into the Unique Self Symphony. Then my love story becomes chapter and verse in the Universe: A Love Story.** Then I'm playing a larger game. Then I'm participating directly in the evolution of love.

We're going to talk about our code; Barbara is going to talk about it, and I'm going to talk about it. But we're also going to introduce a new sacred wild text, which I've been privileged to write, and some of it I did together with another new Taoist friend of mine. It's a gorgeous code that's about touching Reality.

What we're now doing is we are resonating the code with the same chant every week. Our word is *Homo amor*.

- ◆ *Homo amor* is the CosmoErotic Universe in person.
- ◆ *Homo amor* is the new human.
- ◆ *Homo amor* is Unique Self.
- ◆ *Homo amor* is the realization that "I'm a unique expression of the *LoveIntelligence*, *LoveBeauty*, and *LoveDesire* of All-That-Is that can touch Reality in a way that no one that ever was, is, or will be can." That's *Homo amor*.

Amor. The Song of Solomon—in the great ancient texts because we're weaving together all the traditions—he writes, *tocho ratzuf ahava*: its insides are lined with love.

Homo amor. Amor is the center of everything. *Sat-chit-ananda* (in Hinduism, which Sri Aurobindo loved so much, and Barbara loved Sri Aurobindo so much): *sat* is being, *chit* is consciousness, so this means the inside of being consciousness; and *ananda* is love—so the inside of consciousness is love. Love or *amor* is the Inside of the Inside. It's the Holy of Holies. It's the deepest of the deep.

But not ordinary love, not the love which is a strategy for egoic domination, or even for status, or even for superficial security. We're not talking about ordinary love which is limited to the human being. We're talking about Outrageous Love. We're talking about Evolutionary Love, which is the love that moves the Sun and other stars—that's *amor*. *Amor* is at the center.

We chant *Amor* and then we go into prayer, we play our hymn, the holy and the broken *Hallelujah,* and we offer up prayer; we participate with God in prayer. Then we go into the deep *dharma*.

PRAYER: EVERY PLACE YOU FALL, YOU FALL INTO HER ARMS

Oh my god, we're about to go into prayer. So, what is prayer? We think prayer is a cosmic vending machine god that we put in a quarter, and out of that quarter, we get a shiny car. But it's not quite that way. **God is not a cosmic vending machine, as is not owned by one religion that has the only set of prayers.**

God is both the Infinity of Power that flows and drives all Reality, and God is the infinity of creative love that lives in me, as me, and through me. That same creative *LoveIntelligence* and *LoveDesire* that drives Cosmos—that we call God in the third person—lives in me in the first person, but also speaks to me and holds me.

We invoke Rumi, Hafiz, and Kabbalists, and the Cathars, who knew that *every place you fall, you fall into Her arms.* So, God is second person, and second person is not a myth; it's not a mythopoetic rendering. It's a mythopoetic ontology.

We begin to understand this realization, this awakening to the inner truth of Cosmos, which is the personal face of Cosmos. It's the personal beyond the impersonal. *Its insides are lined with love,* but not with generic love, with personal love, or what we call here in our *dharma, intimacy.* **God is not only the Infinity of Power, God is the Infinity of Intimacy that knows my name and cares about every detail.**

Let's do the meditation because we really want to ground the church in these meditations so we can land them in our hearts, so we can awaken to a radical enlightened state, and we can also awaken Reality to this enlightened state; we can begin to invoke a collective enlightenment.

Here's the practice.

We shut our eyes and imagine what we've called God in the third person: billions of light years, running through the cosmos, the infinite complexity of all the supercomputers in the world, exponentialized—supercomputers cannot generate something even vaguely close to photosynthesis.

We have this infinitely complex, gorgeous, dazzling beyond imagination to the nth degree, God in the third person, over trillions, billions, hundreds of billions of galaxies—just in one universe. Then begin to think about a multiverse.

All of that is God in the third person. Imagine it—beyond! It stretches you to the breaking point, you collapse in a puddle of ecstasy before the Divine. All of that is God in the third person.

Now imagine all of *that* sitting in a chair right next to you, looking at you with mad tenderness and mad love, saying, *Oh my God, my beloved, bring before me your holy and your broken Hallelujah!*

That's what we do here. That's what's happening right now. If you really get that right now, and you get on the Inside of the Inside, you can feel it. Right now, that's what's happening.

As we go into Leonard Cohen, be prepared, we're going to offer our prayers. Take us away all the way inside: the Inside of the Inside, the Infinity of Intimacy. "Hallelujah," Leonard Cohen [See Appendix]

Let's lift these prayers to the sky. It is so good, so wondrous, and gorgeous to be together.

I just want to say one thing, then we're going to go into this wild holy movement so we can be here in the church of Evolutionary Love.

- ◆ We are da Vinci in Florence.
- ◆ We are writing the new source code.
- ◆ We are the leading edge of evolution.

We are totally humble; we are imperfect vessels for the light. We are radically committed here. We have a claim to telling the new story. Da Vinci is all of us together.

The moment someone opens their heart, you can feel it. We are one body—utterly distinct, Unique Self Symphony, a unique band of Outrageous Lovers—but we can literally feel the One Heart of Cosmos open; and the source code begins to rewrite itself, but not as long as I'm just spectating: *oh, I'm in church; I'm getting a little moved.*

No, I step in! I put my entire life on the line in evolutionary terms. *Can I open my heart, and can I open it in a new way? Can I go deeper? Can love lift me higher?*

EVOLUTIONARY LOVE CODE: THERE ARE NO EXTERNALITIES

Our crisis is a birth personally and collectively because crisis is an evolutionary driver.

Every great crisis at its root is a crisis of intimacy.

Crisis means that someone or something is being left out of our circle.

Enlightenment means intimacy with all persons and all things.

103

Enlightenment means that there are no externalities.

I want to ask you to shut your eyes for a second, and I want to just share with you this deep take on our code. Today, we're talking about the crisis as *a crisis of intimacy*. Our global intimacy disorder can only be healed through restoring intimacy.

I want to just feel it this way. It's time for an Outrageous Love *revolution*. We are the Outrageous Love Revolution.

Now what's Outrageous Love? Outrageous Love is Eros.

And what's Eros? Eros is the self-evident right to the joy, truth, and beauty that naturally derives from the integrity and goodness of our mutual touch.

We have to touch each other. It's always mutual. It's always full—not just consent, but radical mutuality. And we have to touch each other on all levels. **But what's happened is we lost our trust that touching each other in radical mutuality—either literally, or emotionally, or intellectually— is a value for its own sake.**

- We don't believe we can touch each other.
- We don't believe we can touch Reality.

One of the great tragedies of our time, which comes from Immanuel Kant, is the Neo-Kantian legacy. Kant said there are noumena[11] and phenomena, and we can only touch the phenomena, but we can never actually touch the essence of Reality, noumena. But Kant was wrong for a lot of reasons.

Kant was responding to something from an intellectual legacy, which is the source of the entire disenchantment of Cosmos, which says we can't touch Reality. Kant introduced a strangeness into reality.

So, we became *strange*. We lost the ability to touch ourselves. We began to talk about touching ourselves as jerking off. You get how it's translated?

---

11 *Noumenon* is defined as *a posited object or event as it appears in itself independent of perception by the senses; Merriam-Webster's Collegiate Dictionary*, 11th ed. (Springfield, MA: Merriam-Webster, 2003),

- We lost the ability to pleasure ourselves.
- We lost the ability to pleasure Reality.
- We lost the ability to understand that we have direct holy contact with Reality.

We lost our trust that touching each other in radical mutuality—either literally, emotionally, intellectually, aesthetically, existentially, or psychologically—is a value for its own sake.

We live to touch! Molecules want to touch each other; Alfred North Whitehead called that *prehension*—the desire to touch each other.

We have to restore the faith, which is the way of the erotic activist, that we have the capacity to touch Reality. That's what Reality is: a web of allured touch.

It's only in our ability to touch each other and to touch Reality that we can actually stop Reality from being untouchable.

We know that we're radically loved and our love is radically needed. We know that we're touched by God, and that God yearns for our touch.

As long as we regard the world as untouchable—the terrible inheritance of this Neo-Kantian estrangement from Reality—we can't heal Reality. For Reality can only be healed by our touch.

Is this then a touch quivering me to a new identity? God whispers in our ear. God says, *I need your touch!* Is this then your touch quivering me, God, to a new identity?

To say *I love you* is to say *I need you*.

To be a lover is to know that you are needed, that your touch is ultimately needed by All-That-Is.

That in the holy particularity of your particular situation—

- whether it's to complete a book,
- whether it's to stand in the integrity of your Outrageous Love,
- whether it's to be of devotion in a way that seems to be surprising to you—

... there's a unique risk to take: to be in our integrity, to be in devotion, and *to touch Reality in the way that only I can.* That's what it means to be an Outrageous Lover.

To be an Outrageous Lover is to know that Reality needs your service, which really means that at its depth, **Reality needs your touch.**

That's what Walt Whitman wrote: *Is this then a touch? quivering me to a new identity?*[12]

It's our touch that quivers Reality to a new identity. It's our touch of Reality. It's our erotic activism that moves us from dystopia to utopia.

---

12 Walt Whitman, "Song of Myself," in *Leaves of Grass* (Brooklyn, NY: 1855), sec. 28.

CHAPTER EIGHT

THERE ARE NO DEPLORABLES: EVERYBODY IS INSIDE THE CIRCLE

Episode 138 — June 1, 2019

RADICAL SURPRISE AND AMAZEMENT: WE GET TO PARTICIPATE IN THE EVOLUTION OF LOVE!

This is the moment in church when we set our intention. Our intention is: we are ready to play a larger game; we are ready to participate in the evolution of love. Yes, we are ready!

The idea of participating in the evolution of love is so revolutionary and evolutionary—it is core to the emergence of the new human and the new humanity, which is utterly essential to take us across this eleventh hour, as we stand between dystopia and utopia—**that we can forget what it means.**

I mean, we're participating in evolution. That's a particular structure of consciousness. Just like democracy didn't live in consciousness a thousand years ago. You got burned for suggesting democracy; it was an absurd idea. So we're now going the next step—we're going beyond democracy to what my beloved whole mate Barbara calls *synergistic democracy*. We're moving beyond democracy to synergistic democracy.

We are going to the next level. Synergy means when we come together as evolution itself.

What drives evolution? In our *dharma*, which is the best take on the story of Reality available today, **evolution is the evolution of intimacy.** Intimacy means a whole greater than the sum of the parts, a new emergent. That's what synergy means.

Synergy means when two things come together and something new emerges that wasn't available before, and that produces a new structure of intimacy.

That's what it's about. It's about generating new structures of intimacy. And every crisis is a crisis of intimacy.

To generate a new structure of intimacy, to become something new; that's what a new human can be. **What is a human being? A human being is a configuration of intimacy—exterior and interior.** To generate a new human is to generate a new human with a new worldview and a new self-understanding:

- I'm not just *Homo sapiens sapiens*, I'm *Homo amor*.
- I'm a unique configuration of LoveIntelligence, and evolution moves through me.
- I'm a unique configuration of Evolutionary Love, and as such, I have the capacity—it's my essential right, my essential obligation, and my essential joy—to participate in the evolution of love.

You might say, *Why is he so excited about this? We just said this last week.* Hello, good morning! This is not last week.

The nature of time is that every moment in time is a new quality, a time that never was, is, or will be again—every moment in time.

Hello, this is today! Do we have an *Amen*?

What does *Amen* mean? *Amen*—spelled in Hebrew *aleph, mem, nun*—means, *I trust this moment, and this moment trusts me. Amen* means trust. It means *the trust the moment has in me and my trust in the moment.* When we get up every morning, in one mystical lineage, we say *raba emunatecha*[13]: great is your trust in me, God! **What's God trusting me for? To participate in the evolution of love!**

We are ready, God. We are ready, Universe. We are Ready, Reality. We are ready to tell the new story. We know that you have privileged us to be here in this church at the leading edge of evolution, where we're able to step out of the vagaries—and often oppression—of daily life, and to move past the mortgage and past the insurance and past all of the petty and serious beauty/tragic-comedies of our lives, and *take a seat at the table of history.*

Because history is now being made, when we're before a phase shift unlike any that's ever existed in human history before—with exponential tech and exponential possibility and the potential of *exponential suck*—to borrow my friend Daniel's phrase. **Exponential tech generates exponential suck—we're between dystopia and utopia!**

But we're here, we're ready. We say *Hineni*, I am here; we're here. We're ready to participate in the evolution of love. That's our intention, and with that, we begin church. And we're surprised by it; we don't take it for granted, we're surprised and delighted.

Dopamine receptors start cascading in our brains when we're surprised. When we lose the ability to be in radical amazement before that phrase, *we are ready to participate in the evolution of love*, not only do the dopamine receptors in our brain shut down, but our heart closes. But when we're surprised—*Hineni*, Here I am—we are surprised, and we're delighted.

Amen! We trust this moment, and this moment trusts us.

---

13   Book of Lamentations (Eikhah) 3:23: "They are renewed every morning; great is Your faithfulness."

THERE'S AN ONTOLOGICAL PLURALISM IN A PERENNIAL CONTEXT

We're stepping into the One church. The One Church is not the only church. The One Church means there's One Love and One Heart. And One Church: **we're all part of the one church, and the one synagogue, and the one mosque, and the one world, and the one nation. We're part of The One. But as part of The One, we don't get lost.** As part of The One, we express and emerge as the many.

The language of singularity is multiplicity. There's one *dharma*. Not all *dharmas* are the same. There's one set of laws of inner physics and Reality, and yet that one *dharma* splits and explodes into a thousand different and gorgeous expressions. Those expressions sometimes are atheism.

Sometimes there's an atheism that says, *I'm not willing to buy into the small god that the religion sold me, so I have heresy.* But it's what the mystics called *heresy, which is faith.* Sometimes it's Shamanic, and sometimes it's Aboriginal. Sometimes it's classical Catholicism in its highest and most beautiful form, or gorgeous Judaism, or a form of Lutheranism, or Confucianism, or Taoism, or *Vajrayana* Buddhism, or *Kashmir Shaivism*. But these are all expressions of The One.

The One itself, though, has principles. I want to give you a fancy word, I've been working on this word all week. **There's an ontological pluralism in a perennial context.** What does that mean? It means there are many rivers, those rivers all go to The One, but that One has principles that guide it. Those principles that guide it, that's the *dharma*; that's the new story that we're talking about.

Those principles are not tyrannical, they're the nature of Reality. Just like physics isn't tyrannical, it's the inner physics of Reality. It's not like we all have our different versions of inner physics and *let's sit around in Camp Mystic and Burning Man, and let's talk about our versions.* No, that's not true.

There is an inner physics. And you don't get to talk about the inner physics of Reality unless you're really doing inner physics. Just like you don't get to challenge Richard Feynman's version of physics, or Schrödinger's early formulations, unless you're actually in the physics.

THE NEW STORY IS THE NEW PHYSICS OF REALITY

The new story we're talking about is the new physics of Reality. It's a new story, and today **we desperately need a new story. It's the race to the new story. It can't be words, and it can't just sound good. It has to be grounded in the deepest exterior and interior sciences, and they have to be woven together.** It can't just be a scaffolding, it has to be an actual new physics. That is the single most important challenge in the world today: the new story.

Every week, we say the same thing. But we're surprised. Who are we at this church of Evolutionary Love, this One Church? Not one church in the sense of only, but one in the sense that we're moving towards articulating the shared story. When da Vinci was in Florence facing the Black Death, knowing he couldn't go into every village in Europe, he realized *the thing I need to do is to tell a new story.*

I was talking to Barbara last night, and I miss Barbara Marx Hubbard so much. Barbara made a decision. In the last several years of her life, she said, *This is where I'm going to stand.* She called me and said, *Marc, I'm going to stand with you; we're going to join genius. We're going to be*—what I would call—*whole mates.* We talked four or five times every single day, and she said *this is the place the new story is being told.* She said, *I got the beginning of it with conscious evolution, but I want to find my way to the rest of it.*

Barbara and I, every single day, four or five times a day, in one way or the other, for years, talked to each other about this new story.

What's the new story? It's not enough to name a UN Office for the Future. We have to fill that UN Office for the Future with this new story. At the core of the new story is this *dharma*, or this set of principles.

THE INFINITY OF POWER IS ALSO THE INFINITY OF INTIMACY

I want to give you one principle, which is going to bring us into prayer. The principle is: we live in an Intimate Universe. **The reason Reality exists, according to the best interior sciences, is because the Infinite desires the intimate.**

The Infinite is all-powerful. This is so important: how we hold power. The Infinite is all powerful, whether you call the Infinite *Maʾat*, or you call the infinite *Geist*, or the implicate order, or God, or the Tao, or *Atman is Brahman*. The Infinite is *All Powerful*. But saying *All Powerful* is insufficient. The Infinite says, *I desire the intimate*. Infinity desires intimacy. Feel in: *when I can access my desire for intimacy, I'm directly accessing the Infinite desiring the intimate*.

Now, if you want to approach the Infinite, **if I want to find the Infinite, I have to go into that yearning in me for intimacy and realize that the yearning in me for intimacy participates in the Infinity of Intimacy.** We realize the god you don't believe in doesn't exist. Not the old cosmic vending machine, ethnocentric, homophobic, regressive, body dysmorphic, disassociating, elitist god. Not that god, which every religion said we owned. But there is the truly cosmocentric God, who is the face of the Intimate Universe that knows your name, that knows my name. We call that God, *the Infinity of Intimacy*.

The Infinity of Intimacy wants to know everything about you. The Infinity of Intimacy is the lover with us on the bed late at night, after this incredible four hours of making love when you're spent and exhausted, that cuddles up next to you and says: *Tell me everything, I want to know everything about you.*

Let's just do a little meditation, then we're going to go into prayer. Because in prayer, we turn to the Infinity of Intimacy. **Sometimes people can't access God, but they can access prayer.**

My dear friend, Warren Farrell, who's the greatest writer in America today on boys' issues, wrote a book called *The Boy Crisis*. When I first started talking to him about this new vision of God, he said, "Marc, okay, I get it. I can't quite believe in God, but I totally believe in prayer."

But prayer is God. Prayer means that the human being turns to the Infinity of Intimacy and says: *Can I tell you everything? Can I share with you everything? Can I ask for everything?* And the Infinity of Intimacy hears.

Now you might ask, *Marc, did you just make that up? How do you know that? How do you know the Infinity of Intimacy hears?* I want to ask you to shut your eyes for a second and just ask yourself a question. *Can you hear my voice talking?* Oh, you can.

This is called a *pointing-out instruction.*

What in you hears my voice talking? Well, *my ears.* But not just your physical ears, what else? Well, *my intelligence,* because my ears are a vessel of my intelligence. Okay, so your intelligence hears me talking.

Now you're awesome, but are you the most intelligent person in the entire world? So, if you can hear me, and your intelligence hears me, is it only your intelligence? Is your intelligence separate from the larger field of intelligence? Of course not. Your intelligence participates in the larger field of intelligence. If you can hear me talking, is it possible that the larger field of intelligence can't hear me? We just cut through 2,000 years of theology. It's a very gorgeous pointing-out instruction. **When I pray, the intelligence of Reality—the LoveIntelligence and the LoveDesire and the LoveBeauty of all of Reality—the Infinity of Intimacy hears me.**

What we need to do—as part of articulating the new language—is not leave God behind, but participate in and be held by the Divine. Knowing that **every word, every jot and tittle, every breath you take, every move you**

make, the Infinity of Intimacy is holding you, loving you madly, and just delighting and wanting to meet you, with all of His/Her/Its passion and love. That is the realization of the interior sciences.

We bring our holy and our broken *Hallelujah* before the Divine, and we pray as we do every week. Leonard Cohen, when he went to heaven, joined the One Church; not the only church, The One Church, the One Love, and the One Heart. Take us inside, and we're going to pray with our holy and broken *Hallelujah*, and we're going to ask for everything.

HOW DO YOU PRACTICALLY LOCATE INTIMACY IN YOUR LIFE?

I'm just going to say a couple of sentences on intimacy, then I'm going to turn the microphone to Barbara. *Every crisis is a crisis of intimacy.* The crisis of intimacy means that I have to locate where I am and what my contribution is.

And I have to be in devotion. I want to bring that word together: *devotion.* No one can do it themselves.

I was talking to Barbara last night. Since Barbara passed, which has been only seven or eight weeks, it's been so incredibly intense, writing and sustaining and creating the pieces to carry our work forward.

There's been so much demand that I've barely found time to talk to Barbara. I said to you last night, Barbara, *I'm sorry, I'm working so hard to sustain our vision on so many levels, that we don't even get to talk the way we used to anymore.*

So, Barbara, it's so delightful to welcome you to church.

Our theme for the rest of church today is, how do you actually find this intimacy in your life in a real and practical way?

OPENING THE CIRCLE AND LETTING EVERYONE IN

I do love it open, and it is opening when we love it open! As I was preparing today, I was thinking about *our crisis is a birth,* and to open the circle and let everybody in. I started to do an exercise that I want to share with you, to start opening the circle with people you might know but really dislike personally. Let's open the circle, everybody. If you can find somebody that you have not liked—that you thought to be mean, or cruel, or lying, or cheating, or stealing—open the circle and let them in, and see them in the light of the person who is yearning and longing for more love. Just see them that way.

Then let's open the circle wider, and see if we can bring the political situation in. Let's see if we can bring the Democrats and the Republicans in. Try to feel into those Democrats. Those candidates now, they're giving their lives to try to beat Trump for good reason, and they're all being hit back in very difficult ways, and they're trying not to hit back. Let's say one of them goes up and says: "You know what, as a Democrat, I'm opening my mind, my eyes, my arms, and I'm letting them all in. Because we're all humans, we're on one planet."

Imagine that person makes the most gracious and amazing speech, in all these divisions that are fabricated in order to win, and do come from different points of view, all of which have some good to them. I'm seeing the next level of political leadership. Open our arms, let them all in, and bring them into the holy *Hallelujah* of the spirit of the Evolutionary Church. **The spirit of Evolutionary Love is going through everybody, even the worst criminals and culprits of our society.**

Our church is a holy opening—our arms are so wide. As we're going into this political situation, we've let them all in, and we're playing a role that nobody is fully playing on this planet. It's not just forgiving people. In the end, they say, in the New Testament, that forgiveness goes quantum, and everything forgives everything else. They can't stop forgiving. See, we're at the end times. Either we go down into catastrophe—to climate change, resource depletion, and species extinction—or we're going up towards the evolution of a new world. We happen to be the culture on the cusp of that. But what hasn't happened yet is that any of us have had the power to step out there and open our arms so wide, and let everybody in.

As we do that, imagine all of those who are outside our global circle being included. *Father, forgive them, for they know not what they do.* Feel as you do this, your power as an Evolutionary Lover. You know that beautiful phrase in one of Marc's writings: *God needs me. I am needed, I am unique, I am recognized, and I am adored by the God who's the Creator of us all.* If we walk out into this planetary system, with the power of an agent of planetary evolution, we have crossed over onto the other side of the breakdown; we are breaking through.

Feel the church of Evolutionary Love as the place that takes us the next step on the evolutionary spiral. Can you imagine a way of loving, communicating, and experiencing God's love, so deeply that we would be able to do what Jesus did when he was crucified? *Father, forgive them, for they know not what they do*, as he was killed. Then there was Saturday.

Marc, my favorite day in the whole story is Saturday in the tomb of metamorphosis. Nobody really says, what happened on Saturday? Well, we are on Saturday now. But I never thought of the church being a Saturday church. We need to really acknowledge at this very moment, the Saturday church is the church of metamorphosis, and the crucifixion is what's happening worldwide as people are destroying the climate, the planet, and each other. Then in here is: *Father, forgive them, for they know not what they do.* Let's all be in the Saturday church.

I don't think we really have put forward that metaphor. Meaning that the Saturday church is the church of the metamorphosis of each other and of humanity toward Sunday, the resurrection from the dead. What is that resurrection? When Jesus reappeared and Mary saw him, I knew it was true. I mean, I have the resurrection in my soul. I feel the resurrection as a living potentiality in myself and everyone. I feel the metamorphosis.

If I can just take a jump here: how is the self-organizing universe organizing the universe? It doesn't show up at all; you never see it; there are no big statues for the self-organizing universe. But what is the self-organizing universe, from the Big Bang, all the way on up through the quarks and the electrons? It's the interior of evolution, that is in this most awesome ability of bringing separate parts together to be evermore whole.

Now I am declaring that the Saturday church is the church of the self-organizing universe. In the church of the self-organizing universe, we call upon the self-organizing power that has taken us from quarks to consciousness, asking it to carry us the next step—to open our arms wide enough in this church to let them all in: all the deplorables, including ourselves. **We are dedicating the Evolutionary Church, the church of the Saturday, to the transformation of humanity through the evolution of love, creativity, and awareness of how the self-organizing universe actually works.**

With that, I am really declaring something extraordinarily important.

As we provide resources for this church, we're providing resources for the internal metamorphosis of ourselves, number one; person by person, everybody in this church. But we are also then declaring that this Evolutionary Church is itself entering into the metamorphosis process, which means, as a culture, we haven't quite recognized what it would be like to take on internally everybody in here. That the metamorphosis of the Saturday church is affecting every one of our lives now, so that together, as we bring ourselves evermore closer together, we will understand the resurrection of our culture by being that ourselves.

Lo, he was here, and lo he was there. Lo, I'm in Sunrise. Lo, Marc is in Portland. How did that happen? We are given the power, by the way, through our high technology, to be used operationally for the metamorphosis of our species, from the dying humans to the evolving humanity.

I declare the church of Saturday to be the church of the metamorphosis.

LOVING OUR WAY TO ENLIGHTENMENT

Beloved Barbara, remember this exchange where we talked about the church of Saturday. **For Barbara and me, the church of Saturday meant not just Outrageous Love but outrageous pain. We live in a world of outrageous pain, and the only response to outrageous pain is Outrageous Love.** Its insides are lined with love. We have to love our way to enlightenment. The church of Saturday was a church of Outrageous Love and outrageous pain.

One of the phrases that Barbara used so often, which is so deeply rooted in the lineage says: there's a shattering of the vessels which births the new light—*our crisis is a birth*. Barbara looked at me and said *Our crisis is a birth*, and I looked at Barbara and said, *Then every crisis is a crisis of intimacy*.

That self-organizing universe self-organizes towards higher intimacies through you and me; it's our ability to come together.

Our ability to come together sometimes means to step out of what I think my job is. I think my job is this, *I think I have to do this*. But actually, if I look at the wider field, *what does the wider field need, and can I be intimate with the wider field*? Because every crisis is a crisis of intimacy, and we have a global intimacy disorder. **That's the root of our crisis. We have to heal the global intimacy disorder by evoking a new One-World Church and a new One-World Synagogue.**

We cannot *meditate* our way to enlightenment, but *love* our way to enlightenment. That's *Homo amor*; that's the new human.

If we're not willing to break our hearts wide open every week and find the love that animates Cosmos itself performed in our heart which is the

One Heart, then we won't birth *Homo amor*. **We birth *Homo amor* in ourselves. And I know that we will.** It's always a band that comes together. Sometimes it's a band of twelve, or it's a band of 120, or it's a band of 1200. But it's always a band. It's a few good men and women—from all races and ethnicities, from all over the world—who come together and say: *We're going to do this. We're going to take this on. We're going to feel bigger than people usually feel. We're going to love wider. We're going to love it open!* Those are the words with which Barbara started.

Not only are we going to let into our circle all of the deplorables, but we're going to integrate all the deplorables inside of us and become the One Heart and the One Love.

Solomon said, *its insides are lined with love*—and so the only question is: *how deep is your love?*

Let's build this revolution. It's the Outrageous Love revolution.

CHAPTER NINE

OPENING YOUR HEART IS NOT ENOUGH; NO PART OF YOU SHOULD BE LEFT OUT

Episode 139 — June 8, 2019

WE BECOME THE LEADING EDGE OF EVOLUTION

Welcome everyone, from all over the world. There are some 10,000 of us who have stepped up to the Evolutionary Church around the world.

We're setting our intention in this moment. What's our intention? **Our intention is to play a larger game. Our intention is to participate directly in the evolution of consciousness, which is the evolution of love.**

Now, it's so easy to miss the largeness and the utter sensuality of this mission. I'm in Belgium this week, and I had the privilege of giving a keynote at an organizational economic summit. For the first time, I was able to tell this story here in Belgium, with a close group of friends, the story of what we call *Homo amor*, the emergence of the new human and the new humanity, the realization that nature always brings separate parts together to form a larger whole.

But up till now in history, how did nature do that? Nature did it automatically. Nature wove together diverse strands

121

to create something new. That process is called emergence. And evolution is driven by emergence. But we're now in this new moment. Let's step inside all the way and find this moment. What's the new moment? The new moment is the movement to what Huxley called conscious evolution, and my beloved whole mate Barbara spent her life dedicated to this realization.

It's not that evolution is awakening now through conscious evolution; evolution was always awake. When evolution produced mitosis and meiosis—the most complex processes that every supercomputer in the world couldn't replicate—clearly, evolution wasn't asleep. When we say evolution is awakening, what we mean is that evolution is now awakening through us. **We're actually awakening to the realization that we are—when we're at the leading edge of our potential and realizing our peak self—becoming the leading edge of evolution.**

If you get that realization, your life changes. *When I'm having a peak experience*—meaning I'm getting a glimpse, I'm peeking into my peak, I'm getting a sense of me at my best, when I can actually live my greatness, then at the very edge of my greatness, taking my unique risk, giving my unique gift—*that is evolution awakening*, and I am evolution. Conscious evolution means that evolution becomes conscious in me.

---

*Conscious evolution means that
I become conscious of evolution
happening through me.*

What evolves in evolution? What's the plotline of the evolutionary story? This is core to our *dharma*.

Fact one: Reality is evolution.

Fact two: Reality is relationships; Reality is the drive to intimacy.

Fact three: Reality is the evolution of intimacy.

Fact four: When we say *Reality is evolution*, here's what we mean:

- Reality is not just a fact; Reality is a story.
- But it's not an ordinary story—Reality is a love story.
- It's not an ordinary love story, it's an Evolutionary Love Story. It's an Outrageous Love Story.

What does that mean? Outrageous Love means *the very heart of existence itself pulses with love; the interior feeling of the evolutionary impulse is love.*

That love that shows up in me, that *LoveDesire, LoveIntelligence,* and *LoveBeauty* that shows up uniquely in me, as me, and through me, is the personal face of the evolutionary impulse itself coming awake and alive in me, as me, and through me. **Not only is Reality an Outrageous Love Story, but my life as a leading actor in Reality is a unique Outrageous Love Story.** My life is an Outrageous Love Story, which is chapter and verse in The Universe: A Love Story.

Now, you think that's casual? *Oh, what a nice thing to talk about on a Saturday morning.* If you get that, you are enlightened; that's a promise. That is what enlightenment means, to actually live from that center of gravity, if you get the transmission of that right now. The transmission is not coming from Marc Gafni; it's coming from Reality itself. That's enlightenment.

Now our intention makes sense. What's our intention? Our intention is: **I'm ready to play a larger game**. What's the larger game? Is that just a phrase? Is it just a slogan? No, we're waking up. I'm realizing *I'm playing a larger game*, meaning the evolutionary impulse is moving through me, and *I am ready to align my life,* not with my egoic contraction, but *with the evolutionary impulse.* I'm going to play a larger game, and what is that larger game? *I'm going to participate in the evolution of love.*

How do I participate in the evolution of love?

- I awaken to my true identity as an Evolutionary Lover.
- I'm committing my Outrageous Acts of Love.
- I'm playing my instrument in the Unique Self Symphony.

That's the core, that awakening. That new identity that lives in me, as me, and through me, that's not just *Homo sapiens sapiens,* that is *Homo amor*; this is the birth of *Homo amor.*

Homo amor is an Evolutionary Lover uniquely committing Outrageous Acts of Love that could be committed by no one that ever was, is, or will be other than myself. **I join with others in Unique Self Symphony, and we create a bottom-up self-organizing universe, exploding with joint-matched needs and resources.** A Unique Self Symphony of Planetary Awakening in Love through Unique Self Symphonies.

Now, do you think that vision matters? I will wager my life that that vision matters more than virtually anything else on Earth today. Here's the last step.

---

*The vision and the story that
we hold are where we go.*

But that's not cute. That's not a liberal idea, that's not a conservative idea either. It's the very structure of the Universe itself; the structure of learning.

We actually create Reality through the deepest story and narrative that emerges from the deepest expression of the interior and exterior sciences. That story becomes the strange attractor of my life, and it becomes the strange attractor of Reality.

We create from within that consciousness. We're inspired, we're breathed into being. Every breath we take and every move we make, evolution is watching us and being us and living through us. At the center of everything is *Amor.* It's the love that lives in us, as us, and through us.

PRAYER: RECLAIMING THE GOD THAT KNOWS ME

Thank you! Friends, we're about to go into prayer, and what is prayer? We're here to up-level prayer. Our intention is for the evolution of love. We want to reclaim prayer. To reclaim prayer is to reclaim not only the God that moves through Reality as the forces of physics, chemistry, and biology, to reclaim not only the God who's the center of myself, my essence—the God that lives in me, as me, and through me—but to reclaim the God that speaks to me and that knows me. The laws of physics, that's God in the third person. The God who lives in me, that's God in the first person. But there's a Holy Trinity. There's the second person of God, the God who knows me, not the Santa Claus god, but the actual Infinity of Intimacy.

Here's how you find this. Again, every week, we can just stay on the surface, or we could transform—**a transformation so shockingly amazing that your entire journey in this lifetime changes.** So, if you want to access what prayer is, access the Infinity of Intimacy with me.

EXPONENTIALIZED DESIRE AND EXPONENTIALIZED TENDERNESS

Imagine a moment in which you felt radically tender, like totally wildly tender. It could be to a son, to a brother, to a sister, to a lover or beloved, to a friend. Try and find that moment. You have the most sweet, infinitely tender moment. Now double that moment, make it twice as tender. Triple that moment. Quadruple that moment. 10 times, 100 times, infinite times. You have the tenderness, now we're going to add a piece.

Add the most intense erotic desire you've ever felt for someone in your entire life. Just find it inside. Now double it, triple it, quadruple it. So, we're in meditation. Take these two moments of exponential desire and exponential tenderness, and now weave them together. Then know that *this is how the personal face of God looks at you.*

This is how the personal face of God feels you. That's what we call the Infinity of Intimacy.

The Infinity of Intimacy means that you exponentialize your own experience of desire and tenderness, you weave them together, and you realize this is how the Infinite desires intimacy—not generally; remember, it's not meta-intimacy. Infinity desires intimacy with *you*, and She wants to love *you* open madly. That realization—that's the Infinity of Intimacy.

We turn to the Infinity of Intimacy, our Outrageous Lover that's holding us madly, and we say:

You just made love so unbelievably, and now I know you love me so much.

This is the actual Reality of the Cosmos. It's not a metaphor.

Now, after we've made love, I want to share with you things I've never shared with you, and I want to ask you for your help because I need your help.

Let me share with you my holy and my broken *Hallelujah*.

That's what we're going to do right now. We're going to turn to the Infinity of Intimacy, and we're going to ask for everything. In this moment, the gates are open. To be awake, to be realized, and to participate in the evolution of love is to realize *there's something beyond me, that lives in me that's holding me in every moment.*

She loves me madly, and She desires me beyond imagination.

So, we pray. Let's lift all these prayers to the sky. Let's lift them up to the sky in a way that it's never been lifted to the sky before.

EVOLUTIONARY LOVE CODE: ENLIGHTENMENT MEANS THERE ARE NO EXTERNALITIES

Our crisis is a birth personally and collectively because crisis is an evolutionary driver. Every great crisis at its root is a crisis of intimacy. Crisis means that someone or something is being left out of our circle. Enlightenment means intimacy with all persons and all things. Enlightenment means that there are no externalities.

126

Let's look at our code for a second. Enlightenment means that there are no externalities. What does "no externalities" mean? It means *I do stuff, and it has all these side effects, but I ignore them.* I'm a company, I'm creating my product where I dump stuff in the river, and I ignore the river. But all of a sudden, I realize that everything's on the inside. No one's on the outside; nothing is on the outside.

Every crisis is a crisis of intimacy. **What does a crisis of intimacy mean? It means that something is left out, or someone is left out.**

WHO HAVE I LEFT OUT OF MY HEART?

I was giving a talk yesterday. It was this beautiful program where they told that *you have to go from hard times to heart times*; it was about opening your heart. One thing that I said in this keynote was, *it's not enough to open your heart. Because you can open your heart and leave a lot of people out.* I open my heart for my family. But what about everyone else right in my city, who's starving, who's needy, who's destitute?

Did you know that forty-three percent of Americans cannot support themselves? We have new names for poverty that we use, we call them *income-deprived,* **but they don't have enough money every month to pay for housing, education, food, and phone**—forty-three percent of Americans, even though unemployment just went below four percent.

Here's a crazy secret. For those of you who are from the United States, it's becoming a poor, rich country. Because the level of poverty, the level of desperation, the level of uncertainty, and lack of safety is beyond imagination. But *I don't feel those people because my heart is only open to the people in my circle.*

When I open my heart, who do I need to include that's left out? Sometimes we leave a person out. So, I'm going to ask everyone, *who have we left out of our prayers?* Let's start with just individual people. Sometimes there are people you just leave out; we open our hearts, but not to them. Now, I'm not saying that in your fight with that person, you were wrong. I'm saying you left that person out of your heart.

You can never leave anyone out of your heart. Sometimes you have to be hard. **Sometimes you have to withdraw. Sometimes you have to step back.** *But we never look away.* We can step back, or we can step closer, but we never look away. That's what an Outrageous Lover is; Outrageous Lovers don't look away. Who have I looked away from?

I want to challenge us a little bit today. Can you write the name of a person that you've left out of your prayers or out of your heart? Come on, let's be courageous. Courage means that *I access the fierce timbre and resonance of my heart.* The first step is to recognize whom *have I left out of my heart?*

Here's our practice now, and we're going to do this with the entire world. Every single person who wrote the name of someone that they left out of their heart, will you now step in and write that name again and say, *I'm now bringing that person into my heart.*

- That doesn't mean that they were right.
- That doesn't mean that the issue is resolved. It means I'm now bringing that person back into my heart.
- It doesn't mean you have to give it all up. It means you have to bring that person back into your heart.

The beginning is demonization; we demonize people, and then we dissociate from them, and then we deport them, and then we become violent. One way is, we're verbally violent, we're abusive. In the end, we even get physically violent in terrible ways. But the second I begin the process of demonization, I'm taking someone out of my heart; demons don't have a place in my heart.

YOU CAN'T LOVE A PERSON IF YOU'VE LEFT OTHER PEOPLE OUT OF YOUR HEART

I want to tell you something completely crazy. There's a beautiful teaching in the mystical tradition about the day that a person gets married. Now when I say get married, I mean not only in the traditional sense, even though in the original lineage it was in the traditional sense, but I mean anytime I commit to another person in love. On the day that a person gets married, that day is a day which is called *Yom Kippur. Yom Kippur* is the day of forgiveness and the Day of Atonement.

The question is, why is the day that I get married considered the day of *Yom Kippur?* Now on *Yom Kippur*—on this particular holy day in this particular lineage tradition, which happens to be the Hebrew lineage tradition—what you do on *Yom Kippur* is you forgive people; anyone who's done something to you, you forgive them. You let it go. You give it up. It doesn't mean you take that upon you which is wrong; it means you give up the hatred. You let the person back into your heart.

Here's the teaching—it's so beautiful. You can't love one person if you've left other people out of your heart.

> *You can't love one person if you've left other people out of your heart.*

Isn't that crazy? Every time you leave someone out of your heart, you're cutting off a piece of your heart. There's one love and one heart, and no one's on the outside of my heart. **The second I leave someone out of my heart, I'm devastated, because it's one love and one heart.** So, we brought everyone back into our heart in this beautiful way.

WHAT'S THE PART OF OURSELVES THAT WE'VE LEFT OUT OF OUR HEART?

Now, are you ready to go the next step? Let's drop into one heart together. We're one love and one heart; we're each unique expressions of that great heart. Now let's pour energy into each other, because we affect each other's energy fields.

But that's not hocus-pocus, that's not some human potential or New Age idea, or some Jewish or Christian idea. No, that's true. Reality is arrangements of intimacy. **What's my DNA? My DNA is a pattern of intimacy.** Three billion separate units arranged in a particular pattern of intimacy which encodes information. Information itself is an energetic quality.

We resonate off of each other; we're strings that vibrate off of each other. Let's drop into one heart, let's be the one heart, and let's each be a unique string of the one heart. Now from that place of one heart, I'm going to ask you a second question.

What is the part of ourselves that we've left out of our heart? See, just like we left out other people, there's a piece of ourselves that we've actually left out of our heart.

There's a piece of ourselves that we've split off, that we've disowned, and we can't love that part of ourselves because somehow it's been demonized. But there's no part of ourselves that's not worthy of love. There's no quality that doesn't have at its core a spark of holiness. If you've left out your shame, bring it back in. Because what is my shame? My shame is whispering in my ear, *you're a queen!* That's why you feel shame, because you're a queen; only queens would feel shame. **Your shame is *actually* a secret call to greatness.**

Let's take it from there. Barbara, you and I have done this practice together. I just want to welcome Barbara Marx Hubbard. The veil between worlds is very thin. Barbara, I'm so delighted to welcome you to the Evolutionary Church.

WHEN YOU'RE IN CRISIS, WHAT'S NEW ABOUT YOU IS OFTEN LEFT OUT

This is so vital, so lively. I'm a journal writer, and I'll just share this practice because it's been so powerful for me. I'm on Journal #204. I started when I was 18 years old, and just about every day, I have two ways of writing.

One was the mental: here's what's going on; here's what I'm dealing with.

The other was the deeper self, which is not only the prayer but the deep knowing that's in everybody about what's actually going on. If you allow the mental mind to be quiet, and you tap into the mind that is the expression of the deepest impulse of creation in every one of us—the more that we bring that deepest impulse of creation up to consciousness, as we're doing in the prayer.

That's why it's so important to write it because what I discovered is that writing not only my prayers, but writing what the deeper self knows—that *it won't fully inform me unless I truly ask.*

Ask, and it is given! Knock, and doors are open!

So, I'm saying this double thing with the meaning of the prayer and the meaning of the written word, and the meaning of allowing yourself to write from your deep self when we do the prayer, which I think many of us are doing.

I said I pray for 100% intimacy because I've been thinking a lot about intimacy in the past few days, and I realized that to the degree **I can be 100% intimate, I can be 100% revealed as to who I am, who it is, who the world is to increase intimacy with our beloveds,** such that we can go the whole way with being intimates, out of that comes the newness and the birth of who we are.

Our crisis is a birth. Birth is an evolutionary driver.

The question is, *what's being left out?* Because *the crisis means something is being left out.* Here is the insight I had about what's being left out.

Place ourselves now in the crisis, not only of our own lives, but the crisis of the birth of a new culture, the crisis of the breakdown of the old and the breakthrough of the new. The crisis of climate change, the possible devolution of our species, and the crisis of something jumping.

I don't think it's any accident that our church was formed during the crisis of the birth of humanity, which none of the existing structures have a way of communicating. I mean, the great churches with the great texts of the past had hints of the new, but they projected into another realm altogether. Whereas, here we are, the new.

Here's what I wanted to say with my revelation today. What is being left out in our own personal crisis of birth? Now, it could well be that what's being left out of our crisis of birth is the birth of the new human as ourselves.

In other words, if you really feel that you are an emerging human, and in that sense, you're new, you're not your typical daily person. And what's new about you is very often left out when you feel you're in crisis. **When you're able to reconnect with what is genuinely emergent in you, you are at the same time connecting with the impulse of evolution itself, as you emerging.** In other words, what's emerging is you as an expression of the impulse of creation of universal evolution. That's who you are.

I just had a brief flash of what it feels like to be a fertilized egg. Now we probably can't remember that, but it was really explosive. The first thing that happened with that little tiny fertilized egg, when the sperm enters the egg, is the heart. So, a little heartbeat sound turns on in that little tiny zygote, and as you know, it goes all the way through its developmental history, and it comes out as a new baby. It doesn't like it, and it has struggles, etc. I'm going to say that we, in our generation, could be considered like a cultural baby, born through the womb of evolution into the New Age, the new human, the new church, and the new potentiality of humanity all together.

Let's get what we think this might be, if we were to live through the intimacy of our union with that deeper self coming forward, as what we've been calling *Homo amor universalis*. Maybe what's been left out of so many of us is the actual experience of our newness. Let's feel into *Homo amor*

132

universalis as what's been left out in the crisis of birth, and let's see if we can have a feeling of intimacy with the newness that we are.

I'll just take a second to do that for myself, and for ourselves in this church. In order to be intimate in the crisis of the birth of yourself (which then leads to the birth of everybody else that you're connected with and of the world) and to stay in touch with yourself, during your emergence as a new human, it requires a very deep attention on the experience—both of that inner impulse of evolution that came from the quarks, the electrons, the protons and neutrons, all the way through the genius of evolution, where the new human is being born among *Homo sapiens sapiens.*

All over this planet, I believe new humans are coming forward out of *Homo sapiens sapiens* like us. It's not that we're all great geniuses of the old kind; **we are geniuses of the new kind. And what is the new kind of genius?** *It's the genius of accessing the uniqueness of ourselves and sharing our genius with each other.* Joining genius in supra-sexual co-creation of a world equal to our potential.

What I would like us to just consider here is that the church is the birthplace of this new human. If each of us, right now as members of this church, feeling that we're giving birth to that new human within ourselves, would take time together on this call to just experience anything new that's being born as you. What's new being born in me is *faith*, in the birth. So, what's new that's being born in you that might have been left out of your feeling of being the human that you are becoming? Because if we're becoming, we're new. *Homogeneous, homo-genius, homo-gene-us.*

I'm imagining, if we can just take a little jump here and think of the planetary awakening on planet Earth, and think of ourselves as a microcosm right here of planetary awakening. What does it feel like? It's a vast supra-sexual orgy of joining genius on a planetary scale.

Now, nature has been able to join single cells, to multi-cells, to organisms, all the way up. It's not done just by human will alone; we could not organize 52 trillion cells per person on this TV set talking to each other. But right now, I'm just calling the church, which is dedicated to the vision of a planet awakening in love. In the Teilhard language, *through the noosphere, getting its collective eyes, through us being able to see each other on that vast internet.*

I'm adding that each person is going to be invited to give the gift in such a way that the universe's self-organizing system is going to help us find where the gift is most needed, most loved, most wanted, and where it fits best. Let's celebrate a planetary crisis of the birth of the new human, *Homo amor universalis,* self-organized through a self-organizing universe. And our church is its first overt birthing place.

WE ARE THE PEOPLE TELLING THE NEW STORY

Friends, this church cannot stop where it is now. This church has to get to a place where there are one million, two million, and three million people around the world who are tuned into Evolutionary Churches around the world, and this church itself holds 50,000–60,000 people a week. That's what it should be in order to impact the source code of culture.

We are the people telling the new story. This is not cute; this is about a *supra-sexual* orgy of co-creation, as Barbara said. **But what does supra-sexual mean? It means Eros. It means our unique, gorgeous creativity with nothing left out of ourselves steps up, and we become the Unique Self Symphony. We are the tellers of the new story.** If you think this new story we're telling is being told everywhere, *no.* In some sense, we are the hub of this new story. It's a stunning responsibility. It's a stunning obligation. It's a stunning joy.

Barbara, I miss you. You were just the most unbelievable whole mate, and you continue to be so, and we resonated so deeply with that same evolutionary impulse. Oh my God, it's so great to have you with us. *How can anyone ever tell you that you're anything less than beautiful? How can anyone ever tell you that you are less than whole?*

This is the Evolutionary Church. This is grassroots. This is bottom-up. This is the self-organizing universe. From around the world, Outrageous Love to everyone. This is the Outrageous Love revolution, it's happening here; we are it. We love each other madly. Let's build, and together we come, and we raise it to the next level next week. *Hallelujah,* everyone!

CHAPTER TEN

CONSCIOUS EVOLUTION: A LOVE STORY

Episode 140 — June 15, 2019

POISED AT THE ABYSS, WE ARE CALLED TO EVOLUTION

We are, friends, the articulators in this generation, this generation which is unlike any other generation that has ever existed in history. We have within us the capacity that has never existed. We went from half a billion to seven billion and climbing, on an exponential growth curve. This explosion of technology has brought us to a place where we have both the capacity to create heaven on earth, to create resources, abundance, depth, goodness, truth, and beauty, unlike Reality has ever seen. **Or, we stand—literally poised at the abyss—before a potential dystopia, which is rapidly and imminently approaching.** Because this exponential growth curve falls off, like all growth curves do. And, we have this explosion of exponential tech, which also creates exponential danger. And we have a list of existential risks that threaten Reality in a way that has never existed before in the history of the human race. **We're—at this moment—poised between dystopia and utopia.**

---

*But we are confident because we
know that nature moves as separate
parts to become larger wholes. We
know that this is the way of evolution.*

And, this is the place where Barbara and I met. We both believed in this notion of conscious evolution. I got it from the Hebrew mystics, and I got it from Kook. They downloaded into the Christian *Kabbalah* of the Renaissance which then went to Fichte and Schelling. And Barbara got it from de Chardin and other places, and we both deepened it in our own ways.

We met in conscious evolution, and then we added a piece—but it's a crucial piece. **That crucial piece is a love story, what I would call the Universe: A Love Story.** And I just want to share with you an intention.

WE'RE BRINGING THE NEW GOOD NEWS

I had a dream this week, and in that dream, Barbara and I had this fantastic conversation. In this dream, Barbara and I were talking about what the future holds.

Where are we going with the Evolutionary Church? Where are we going with the Center for Integral Wisdom, and with the Foundation for Conscious Evolution?

Here's the sentence that came down in the dream, which really brings together for me the last 2,000 years of work that brings together all of our work—**conscious evolution: A Love Story.** Those are not separate. *That's what this church is.* This church understands that the response to existential risk must be a new story, although all the infrastructural responses are necessary. We need to redesign civilization, and that's utterly essential, but that redesign can't just be technical, structural. It needs to reflect the new story.

If you think that's a casual sentence, it's not. This is literally the single most potent and powerful thing we can do on the planet today to move us towards the transformation of suffering, to move us toward the place where *every child knows* that:

- I'm a Unique Self.
- I have a unique contribution to make to the Unique Self Symphony.
- I'm a unique configuration of love and intimacy ultimately needed by All-That-Is.
- I am evolution!

That realization is: the birth of every human being, which is the very evolution of God—God the Lover who lives *through* everything and animates all of Reality.

That realization is the Good News. It is the Gospel, if you will, of this Evangelical church. And, yes, we are an Evangelical church in the sense that *we're bringing the Good News.* And we have to liberate the grasp of the fundamentalist community.

They have so many important things to say but they're bringing us yesterday's news, and yesterday's news is that God is an ethnocentric god, and only a particular path will allow you to be redeemed—whether it's a Southern Baptist path or a Pentecostal path—that *if you don't believe in that particular way you're damned to eternity.*

No, that's the old news, that's the old news.

We're bringing the new Good News. The new Good News is the evolution of love.

In the evolution of love, we understand that we're going to *actually participate* in that evolution. We are the *dharma*, we are the new story. It's our obligation, our privilege, our responsibility, our duty, our honor, our delight, and our devotion to stand at the brink of devastation and speak the word: *Let there be light.* **Let there be light means *let there be a new story*.**

The word story in Hebrew, *sippur*, also means the new resplendent light. *Sappir* is the blue light in meditation of the new story. So, *sappir*, the new light, is the new story *sippur*, which is the best version of Evolutionary Love, of conscious Outrageous Love.

This is the Gospel church of the new civil rights movement, but in this new civil rights movement, it's not only that all people are born *equal*. It's that **all people are born *creative*—as creative expressions of that Evolutionary Love—and that each of us are needed, no one's extra, and everyone is God incarnate.**

We set our intention, as we do every week, and we declare it to be true: to play a larger game. We have to participate in *Homo amor*, the new humanity, and the new species. *Amor* is the center of everything. Conscious Evolution: A Love Story.

That's our new sentence, this Conscious Evolution: A Love Story. And I actually haven't had that clear of a kind of revelation dream since 2006–2007. Just feel it, Conscious Evolution: A Love Story. That's the new book. That's the *dharma*. And it summarizes everything we've been saying. Conscious Evolution: A Love Story.

EVOLUTION IS THE EVOLUTION OF INTIMACY

And intimacy is shared identity in the context of otherness. We come together to share an identity.

Quarks are driven by allurement to come together, and they share an identity: Quarks combine to form protons, electrons, neutrons. Quarks come together, and they form subatomic particles. Subatomic particles come together, and they create a shared identity; they're driven by allurement. They create a new intimacy which is called an atom.

Intimacy drives the story. Atoms come together, and they form a molecule. There's this drive, this allurement, this Eros, that moves Reality to come together in a new shared identity. That goes all the way up the evolutionary chain until we have the One Church of Evolutionary Love, which is us coming together, creating a new identity as part of this.

We don't lose our old identity. We are all individuals; we're all Unique Selves, but we're forming this larger community. We can feel each other.

Intimacy equals shared identity; we have a shared identity (in the constant of otherness we maintain our radical individuality) plus mutuality of pathos (we can feel each other) and mutuality of purpose. What's our purpose? To tell the new story, to stand in this place between utopia and dystopia, at this abyss, and tell the new story, and to heal and to transform.

WHAT'S THE SOURCE OF ALL THIS? WHERE DOES THIS DRIVE FOR INTIMACY COME FROM?

This drive for intimacy comes from the Infinite. The Infinite desires the finite. The infinite God wants intimacy. And God/Goddess is the Infinity of Intimacy.

At this moment, we turn to God, not to the god you don't believe in who doesn't exist—not to the god who's ethnocentric, homophobic, owned by one religion, and is running a private cosmic vending machine where you put in a prayer and get out a shiny car—but God who is the Infinity of Intimacy, who loves us madly, yearns for us, holds us, and audaciously loves us open. The Christian nuns wrote about this in the sixteenth century: *Jesus, love me open.*

Return to the Infinity of Intimacy that knows every detail of our lives, every desperation, every contraction, every hurt, and every trauma, and holds us, holds the holy and the broken *Hallelujah.*

EVOLUTIONARY LOVE CODE: LOVE IS NOT MERELY AN EMOTION; LOVE IS A PERCEPTION

Love is not merely an emotion. Love is a perception.

To be a lover is to see with God's eyes.

To be a lover is to love the moment open. And we love the moment open by seeing with God's eyes.

We're all connected. Let's say we have a great conversation at some depth with our hearts open; then the code comes down, and they're completely related. **It's the way that we love each other, it's the way that we're a band of Outrageous Lovers together, that allows the codes to open up.**

We're building a Great Library together, but we are the Great Library; we are the *dharma*.

Let's look at this code, and I want to code it with you, together. I want to be with you, Barbara, and feel everyone.

What's happened over the last four years? We had an explosion of *dharma* in the last forty years in my world; I started doing *dharma* some forty years ago. And Barbara had another twenty years before me, and then we brought these memes together, and something exploded in the world that we all need to land together.

We're going to take this to the next step. Barbara, you came to me five years ago and said: *Marc, I know you're going to know how to do this. I've read everything you've written, and I want to bring these moves together. And this is the next step.*

And, you saw it before I did, and I promised you then, I promised you in the hardest of times, and in the most beautiful times, that we were totally committed to this, and that we would stay in this until this new story was *told from every hilltop and under every leafy tree*, as the Bible says. And this new story becomes part of the very source code of culture, the very source code of humanity.

And that we would together, all of us together, be the new da Vinci, who was in Florence, who stood in the face of the abyss of the Black Death and in the destruction of Europe and knew that only a new story could take us the next step.

We are exponentialized in that situation, and we are here together. And, Barbara, it's an absolute promise. We are in, we are in all the way. Nothing left out. This code is so wildly important:

Love's not merely an emotion; love is a perception.

There's a lot to say about that on the interpersonal level.

When I was in Dharamsala hanging out for a wild day with the Dalai Lama in his room at his private home, we'd had an argument, which is a wild story that some of you know. (We had met in the summer home of the Pope a little while before then.)

I gave him my *yarmulke*, my skullcap, and he took the *yarmulke* back with him to Dharamsala. He sent me a message: *If you want your yarmulke, come to Dharamsala and get it.* So, I went to Dharamsala to get my skullcap, my Jewish ritual garment. We had a fantastic day there.

There was a moment in that conversation, the public part of the conversation, where we were talking, we said, "Love is not an emotion. Love is a perception." This code. He got so excited, and the Dalai Lama has that beautiful way of getting excited, saying, "Beautiful, beautiful, beautiful," because what it means is: if love is just an emotion, it's energy in motion—

it hits you, you get hit by Cupid's arrow, it's coming from outside you, you're lovestruck, you're blinded by love, something's happening to you, you're filled with an emotion

—then it fades, the energy fades and dies, and then you're stuck without love: you're in a loveless marriage, or a loveless life, or a loveless relationship, because you can't access that first burst of energy, that first burst of enthusiasm, that first arousal. You can't find it anymore.

My friends, tragically, that's true for most people because we make love very small.

I SEE YOU WITH GOD'S EYES

We make love ordinary, this experience between human beings. We make love merely an emotion. Love is an emotion but it's an emotion that emerges from a perception. Perception is a capacity that we have: we're active, we're not waiting for love to happen to us; we're training our perception. **If we can cleanse the doors of perception, all we see is the Infinite.**

If I cleanse the doors of perception, **I don't see you in your brokenness. I hold the beauty of your brokenness, and your brokenness is but a door to your light.** I realize that your broken heart is whole and that there's nothing more whole than your broken heart. I see you in your infinite beauty. I see you in your Unique Self and in the unique expression of the Divine that's incarnate in you.

Love is a Unique Self perception. But it's even more than that. To be a lover, says the code, is to see with God's eyes. I see you with God's eyes. I see you the way God sees you. Love is not really an emotion; it's a perception. And to be a lover is *we see each other with God's eyes*. Now, let's take it the next step.

Here's a practice—which I shared with Barbara, and it's very beautiful. In the mystical tradition, we move from what's called in the tradition, *mi'tzideinu* to *mi'tzido*. We move from our perspective to God's perspective. Let's slow the whole thing down. We move from our perspective to God's perspective. Can you feel that?

Actually, I begin to see with God's eyes. Not only do I see you with God's eyes, but I see all of Reality with God's eyes. Can you feel that?

I see from the divine perspective. I see the entire evolutionary story; I see the story from the very beginning.

And I realize that love is… here's the phrase in the mystical tradition: *there's love after creation*. It's beautiful; that's the love which is the beautiful love that appears as romantic love, as the ordinary, gorgeous, extraordinary love between human beings. **But there's *love before creation*. The love before creation is the Outrageous Love that initiates Reality itself. It's the unmanifest starting to become manifest. It's the Infinite desiring the intimate.** That's love before creation.

God's the lover in the whole story. Barbara and I shared the conscious evolution meme, which we got from different places. She spent her life dedicated to a particular expression of Julian Huxley's conscious evolution, and I shared this very deep understanding, which she was ecstatic about. We joined it together: Reality is a love story.

Quarks and particles are all joined together through love. The core quality at the center of Reality is allurement. Allurement brings molecules together, as complex molecules and cells together as multicellular. The single-celled life that was driven by a crisis of intimacy decided, "Oh my God, we have to love each other," and multi-cellular life emerged.

We are able to see from God's perspective, and we're able to realize from God's perspective that the entire evolutionary story is a love story. And we are personally implicated in that story, and at this very particular time and moment in history. **History is the story; it's her-story and his-story. His-story, it's the story we can hold as the whole story.**

WHEN I SEE WITH GOD'S EYES, I CAN SEE THE NEXT STEP IN THE EVOLUTION OF LOVE

To see with God's eyes is to realize I'm not separate from God.

I'm a unique configuration of Evolutionary Love. **God breathed me into existence and, therefore, I can see with God's eyes because just like God is evolution, I am evolution.**

Because I'm a unique incarnate expression of the Divine, because I am evolution, I can see the whole story, I can feel the whole story. So, at this moment in history—**as we stand between dystopia and utopia—I want to know as God, as a conscious co-creator with God, as a unique expression of conscious evolution:** *What is the next step in the evolution of love?* Let's feel that now, let's feel it. But that's not words, it's not a metaphor, it's true.

Let's say together:

> I am evolution.
>
> I am evolution, as evolution, I can see with God's eyes.
>
> Therefore, the entire story is visible to me.
>
> I know what the next step in the evolution of love is.

We now move from joining genes to joining genius. We move from just being soul mates to being *whole mates*. Whole mates means that *it's not just about me*. We joined together, and we're not just Unique Self, *Unique Self as I'm doing my Unique Self in the world*. We create Evolutionary Love WeSpace. We join genius, we become whole mates, and we create a Unique Self Symphony.

We're in devotion not just to our own gifts. You hear this? This is so critical. One of the mistakes in Unique Self is that *I'm always doing my unique creativity*. Sometimes to live my Unique Self is to join a "Unique We" and to give up some of my unique gifts.

When the State of Israel was founded, you had doctors, lawyers, professors, who were turning the swamps of Israel into beautiful, lush fields that could support life. And they were standing in that place of *taking this country and turning it into this in-gathering of the exiles* after the Holocaust. And they stopped doctoring, they stopped lawyering, and they stopped professoring, because that's not where Reality needed them at that moment.

It's very deep. To join genius, isn't just *I bring my particular Unique Self gifts*. It means *I'm in devotion. I see with God's eyes. I say, "What's needed at this moment?"*

GOD'S PERSPECTIVE OF US AT THIS MOMENT OF EVOLUTION

Beloved Marc and beloved everyone, as I'm reading all your prayers, and my prayers, and our prayers, I'd like to take God's perspective for a moment. This is a love story, and God is the Original Lover who is activating this love story in every one of us.

I have always had this perspective deep inside my soul, which is looking back before the Big Bang, into the universal process of creation itself, eternally present.

Then, that impulse—the first impulse in the love story—out of the field comes the force, which is what we're feeling in us now. That force out of the field of eternal, universal consciousness is the same force that was so exquisitely designed in those first three seconds—the Big Bang in which energy, matter, and life were given their original structure.

We're now feeling God's infinite coming into the Big Bang and the power of love alive in us all these billions of years later.

Let's take it from that love that was able to structure it all immediately in a few seconds.

Then, let's allow ourselves to go with God through the quarks being attracted to the quarks, the electrons to the electrons, the protons, the cells, the multi-cells, and let's feel the allurement as the center and source of the multi-billion years from the Big Bang.

Think of that love that attracted every single particle to every other particle to create newness through what we're now calling vocational arousal.

So, we can imagine the quarks, the electrons, the protons, the single cells, running out of energy in the seas of Earth, suddenly realizing they have to be attracted to each other to gain that solar energy and to repopulate the entire world through reproduction.

Through joining together to reproduce each other, eventually it became reproduction through love. It became sexuality. What an amazing gift on just this one planet. Not only to keep all of the rest of life alive, but to reproduce the human species through love and through the most awesome process.

I'm joining genes with an egg that then starts to flourish itself as a person that is you. That actually went through in the womb the entire story of creation. From being a single cell to being a multi-cell to being a little animal to being a little fish, and all of that.

And now it pops out as you, with all of that coded inside you, and you have to be a child, and you go through all of that, and you go through your childhood, and then you go through the stage that we're at now.

And I'd like to just experience ourselves from the origin of creation at this key point in human evolution on this planet when it's perfectly obvious that our planetary system cannot continue to grow as it has been growing, and **it's produced a set of humans at this exact shift point when God the Creator had to create the co-creators.**

If we're going to take it like those single cells that became multi-cells—if we're going to take it from the devolution of our species to that quantum jump to the evolution of our species—what's happening to God inside us if God is the lover going through the entire process of creation?

And, let's now tune into God at the exact moment when each of us can say:

> *I am evolution becoming conscious of itself.*
> *I am God-creator, becoming co-creator.*
> *I am filled with that unique creativity that has within it*
> *the power of the entire story, the Big Bang, all the way on up.*

As Marc says, it's *The Universe: A Love Story.* That's a beautiful sentence, and if you try to see that as a management issue for God, when He's coming forth *as* you, what I'd like to share is:

How is God most clearly showing up now as you, at the threshold of devolution, our evolution, and conscious evolution?

This is the first church of evolutionary consciousness come alive, the first time ever, as far as I know—**the Church of Co-creation of Conscious, Evolving Love**.

FIND THE FORM OF JOINING GENIUS

And to add to this, in order for our evolutionary uniqueness to fully manifest itself, we have to find the form of *joining genius*. We have to, just like we had to find the form to join genes, tell this remarkable story that was able to create all of our lives.

I believe **we are now involved in a story and a discovery as great as the discovery of sexuality. Which is the discovery of supra-sexuality of the lovers that each of us is,** finding the genius that is more precisely capable of then evolving you, and me, and us, into new humans.

We don't get to be conscious evolutionary new humans as individuals alone.

The joining of genius in Evolutionary Love is a manifestation of your genius code, not just your genetic code—everybody's genius code uniquely their own joining with somebody else's genius code uniquely their own—creating a fusion of *mimetic* rather than *genetic* coding to create in you and me and us a new human, a new culture through love, the love of joining genius.

The entire love story (as in some respect the pinnacle of us alive now) is the joining of that genius to create the new.

APPENDIX: SONGS

THE BATTLE HYMN OF THE REPUBLIC—JULIA WARD HOWE[1]

Mine eyes have seen the glory of the coming of the Lord.

He has trampled down the vintage
where the grapes of wrath are stored.

He has loosed the fateful lightning
of his terrible swift sword.

His truth is marching on.

HOW COULD ANYONE—LIBBY RODERICK[2]

How could anyone ever tell you
you were anything less than beautiful?

How could anyone ever tell you
you were less than whole?

How could anyone fail to notice
that your loving is a miracle—
how deeply you're connected to my soul?

---

1 Julia Ward Howe, The Battle Hymn of the Republic, 1862.

2 Libby Roderick, "How Could Anyone," on *If You See a Dream* (Turtle Island Records, 1990), CD.

I WANT TO KNOW WHAT LOVE IS—FOREIGNER[3]

I've gotta take a little time,
a little time to think things over.
I better read between the lines,
in case I need it when I'm older.
(Whoa, ooh-ooh, ooh-ooh)

And this mountain, I must climb
feels like the world upon my shoulders,
and through the clouds, I see love shine,
it keeps me warm as life grows colder.

[Pre-Chorus]
In my life, there's been heartache and pain.
I don't know if I can face it again.
Can't stop now, I've travelled so far
to change this lonely life.

[Chorus]
I wanna know what love is.
I want you to show me.
I wanna feel what love is.
I know you can show me.
Oh, oh-oh, oh (ooh)

I'm gonna take a little time,
a little time to look around me.
I've got nowhere left to hide,
it looks like love has finally found me.

[Pre-Chorus]

[Chorus]

[Outro]

(And I wanna feel) I wanna feel what love is

---

3   Foreigner, "I Want To Know What Love Is," recorded November 1984, on *Agent Provocateur*, Atlantic Records, vinyl LP.

(And I know) I know you can show me.
Let's talk about love.
(I wanna know what love is) The love that you feel inside.
(I want you to show me) And I'm feelin' so much love.
(I wanna feel what love is) No, you just cannot hide.
(I know you can show me) Yeah.
I wanna know what love is (Let's talk about love).
I want you to show me, I wanna feel.
(I wanna feel what love is) And I know, and I know.
I know you can show me (Yeah).
(I wanna know what love is) (I wanna know)
(I want you to show me) I wanna know, I wanna know, wanna know.
(I wanna feel what love is) (I wanna feel)
(I know you can show me).

HALLELUJAH—LEONARD COHEN[4]

Now, I've heard there was a secret chord
that David played, and it pleased the Lord.
But you don't really care for music, do you?
It goes like this, the fourth, the fifth,
the minor fall, the major lift.
The baffled king composing Hallelujah.

[Chorus]

Hallelujah, Hallelujah,
Hallelujah, Hallelujah.

Your faith was strong, but you needed proof.
You saw her bathing on the roof.
Her beauty and the moonlight overthrew you.
She tied you to a kitchen chair,
she broke your throne, and she cut your hair,
and from your lips she drew the Hallelujah.

---

4 Leonard Cohen, "Hallelujah", Various Positions, Columbia Records, 1984, LP.

[Chorus]

You say I took the name in vain,
I don't even know the name,
but if I did, well, really, what's it to you?
There's a blaze of light in every word,
it doesn't matter which you heard,
the holy or the broken Hallelujah.

[Chorus]

I did my best, it wasn't much.
I couldn't feel, so I tried to touch.
I've told the truth, I didn't come to fool you.
And even though it all went wrong,
I'll stand before the Lord of Song
With nothing on my tongue but Hallelujah.

OM NAMAH SHIVAAYA

Om Namah Shivaaya
Shivaaya namaha,
Shivaaya namah om
Shivaaya namaha, namaha Shivaaya
Shambhu Shankara namah Shivaaya,
Girijaa Shankara namah Shivaaya
Arunaachala Shiva namah Shivaaya

*I bow to the soul of all. I bow to my Self. I don't know who I am,
so I bow to you, Shiva, my own true Self. I bow to my teachers
who loved me with love. Who took care of me when I couldn't
take care of myself. I owe everything to them. How can I repay
them? They have everything in the world. Only my love is mine
to give, but in giving I find that it is their love flowing through
me back to the world…I have nothing. I have everything. I want
nothing. Only let it flow to you, my love… sing!*

153

INDEX

A

abandon, 36
abracadabra, 84
abyss, 21, 45, 46, 137, 141, 143
alive, xii, xix, 3, 5, 11, 17, 18, 26, 27, 29, 30, 31, 65, 78, 123, 147, 148, 149
All-That-Is, xxvii, 25, 65, 93, 100, 106, 139
allurement, xv, xxxiv, xxxvi, 83, 140, 141, 145, 147
amen, 60
ananda, 100, 101
Ark of the Covenant, 77
arousal, xxi, 3, 56, 67, 143, 147
atom, xxxvi, 141
atomic, 85
attraction, 83
awaken, xxvii, 45, 48, 89, 90, 95, 102, 123
aware, 8, 51

B

Babylonian Talmud, 31
beauty, xxiv, 4, 35, 80, 104, 109, 137, 144, 153
Bethlehem, 32, 47
Big Bang, 6, 62, 83, 89, 117, 147, 148
blood, 97
Brahman, 112
brain, 109
breath, 114, 124
Buddhism, xvi, 110
bypass, 16

C

calling, xxi, 33, 70, 97, 132, 134, 147, 173
capacities, 174
Cathars, 101
Catholic, 77
Center for World Philosophy and Religion, iv
chain, xxxv, 141
chant, 64, 73, 75, 76, 77, 78, 81, 90, 100, 101
chariot, 38, 42
children, 39, 55, 56
chit, 100
Christ, 41, 49, 69, 81
Christianity, 38, 49, 79, 91
Church, vi, xi, xxi, 1, 2, 4, 6, 7, 8, 9, 17, 29, 31, 32, 33, 34, 38, 40, 42, 47, 52, 60, 64, 69, 73, 75, 78, 79, 80, 90, 98, 110, 111, 114, 115, 117, 121, 130, 135, 138, 141
circle, xxv, 25, 70, 94, 95, 96, 97, 104, 115, 116, 119, 126, 127
clarity, xii, 4, 55
co-creator, 4, 16, 146, 148
collapse, xvi, xxvi, xxvii, xxx, xxxi, xxxii, xxxiii, 102
commit, 48, 55, 56, 100, 129
commitment, 15, 55
communion, xiv, xxxviii, 2
community, xii, 32, 40, 52, 80, 139, 141
complex, xvi, 15, 37, 51, 102, 122, 145
complexity, xvi, 8, 52, 74, 102
confession, 18, 63

connecting, 132
Conscious Evolution, i, iii, iv, xi, xx, xxi, 8, 22, 42, 53, 62, 111, 122, 137, 138, 140, 145, 146, 148, 173, 174
consciousness, xvi, xix, xx, xxii, xxiv, xxviii, 3, 5, 8, 11, 12, 13, 17, 22, 23, 26, 37, 44, 47, 50, 52, 53, 65, 71, 86, 91, 97, 100, 101, 107, 121, 124, 131, 147, 149, 173, 174
continuity of consciousness, xxviii, 3, 5, 11, 12, 13, 17, 22, 23, 26, 50
contraction, 123, 141
conversation, xxi, xxviii, 18, 49, 138, 142, 143
cosmocentric, xvi, 70, 112
cosmocentric intimacy, 70
CosmoErotic Universe, xx, 100
Cosmos, xiii, xiv, xvi, xix, xxv, xxvii, xxxv, 8, 23, 34, 35, 43, 49, 64, 70, 74, 77, 78, 81, 83, 85, 89, 90, 91, 92, 101, 103, 105, 119, 126, 173
creating, 8, 31, 32, 67, 86, 114, 127, 141, 149
creation, xvi, xx, xxi, 8, 21, 52, 83, 131, 132, 134, 145, 147, 148, 149
creative, xxi, xxix, xxxvii, 8, 19, 74, 101, 140
creativity, xxiv, 21, 34, 52, 65, 68, 74, 81, 117, 134, 146, 148
Creator, 116, 148
crisis of intimacy, xxxv, 93, 94, 96, 103, 104, 108, 114, 118, 126, 127, 145
culture, xiii, xvi, xxii, xxiv, xxix, xxx, xxxv, 44, 64, 69, 86, 116, 117, 132, 134, 142, 149, 173, 174

D

Day of Atonement, 129
death, xxviii, xxix, xxx, xxxv, 2, 4, 5, 23, 30, 36, 54, 69, 97
death of humanity, xxx, 69

deepest heart's desire, 20, 25, 38, 50, 63
delight, 2, 9, 23, 31, 62, 66, 71, 73, 90, 140
democracy, 84, 107
depression, 16
desire, xxxii, xxxviii, 4, 14, 19, 20, 23, 25, 26, 37, 38, 39, 48, 50, 52, 54, 55, 56, 63, 71, 81, 83, 84, 105, 112, 125, 126
dharma, xii, 6, 7, 13, 30, 38, 39, 40, 46, 74, 80, 96, 102, 108, 110, 112, 122, 140, 142, 173
dignity, 44, 92
distinct, xxxv, xxxvi, 103
Divine, 8, 9, 34, 35, 37, 49, 71, 102, 114, 144, 146
divinity, 17
dogma, xii, xiii, 7, 46
dreams, 10

E

Earth, xxvi, 33, 44, 54, 68, 97, 98, 124, 133, 147
Eastern, 74
economics, xxxviii
ecstasy, 47, 90, 99, 102
Eden, 76
ego, 17, 44
egocentric, 69, 70
Egypt, 39
electromagnetic, 83
emerge, 63, 97, 110
empower, 52
emptiness, xxxii, 16
emunatecha, 109
enlightenment, xxxviii, 74, 92, 95, 97, 102, 118, 123, 126
Eros, xv, xvi, xvii, xx, xxv, xxvi, xxvii, xxxii, xxxiv, xxxvi, 21, 25, 37, 51, 62, 64, 65, 84, 85, 91, 92, 97, 104, 134, 141, 173
erotic, xxxvii, 35, 105, 106, 125, 174
ethnocentric, xiii, 49, 70, 91, 112, 139,

141

ever deeper, xxvii, 65

evil, 48

evolution, xiii, xiv, xvi, xx, xxi, xxiii, xxiv, xxv, xxix, xxxv, xxxvii, xxxviii, 7, 8, 13, 14, 15, 23, 24, 42, 43, 44, 46, 47, 51, 52, 53, 54, 55, 62, 63, 65, 67, 70, 71, 77, 79, 81, 89, 90, 94, 95, 96, 98, 99, 100, 103, 107, 108, 109, 116, 117, 121, 122, 123, 124, 126, 132, 133, 137, 138, 139, 140, 145, 146, 147, 148, 174

   of consciousness, xvi, xix, xxii, xxiv, xxviii, 3, 5, 11, 12, 13, 17, 22, 23, 26, 50, 97, 101, 107, 121, 174

   of intimacy, xxv, xxvii, xxxiii, xxxv, xxxvi, xxxvii, 7, 25, 34, 35, 48, 61, 65, 66, 77, 78, 81, 84, 93, 94, 95, 96, 103, 104, 108, 112, 114, 118, 122, 126, 127, 130, 133, 140, 145

   of love, xxiii, xxiv, xxv, xxvi, xxxvii, xxxviii, 42, 43, 44, 45, 46, 62, 65, 79, 89, 91, 96, 98, 99, 100, 107, 108, 109, 117, 121, 123, 124, 126, 130, 139, 140, 145, 146, 147

Evolutionary, vi, xi, xii, xviii, xix, xx, xxi, 1, 2, 4, 5, 6, 7, 8, 9, 11, 12, 13, 17, 25, 26, 29, 31, 33, 34, 37, 40, 42, 44, 45, 46, 47, 48, 52, 60, 62, 64, 65, 67, 68, 69, 73, 75, 79, 80, 81, 90, 96, 98, 101, 103, 108, 111, 115, 116, 117, 121, 123, 124, 130, 134, 135, 138, 140, 141, 145, 146, 149, 173

   chain, xxxv, 141

   Church, vi, xi, xxi, 1, 2, 4, 6, 7, 8, 9, 17, 29, 31, 32, 33, 34, 38, 40, 42, 47, 52, 60, 64, 69, 73, 75, 78, 79, 80, 90, 98, 110, 111, 114, 115, 117, 121, 130, 135, 138, 141

existential risk, xxiv, xxviii, xxix, xxxii, xxxiii, xxxiv, xxxv, xxxvi, xxxvii, 79, 138

exterior sciences, xiii, 61, 92, 124

Eye

   of humanity, xvii, xxi, xxix, xxx, 2, 24, 31, 53, 60, 69, 116, 117, 132, 142, 174

F

faith, 8, 35, 105, 110, 133, 153

false self, 62

features, xviii, 84

feminine, 4, 16

feminism, 45

field, xxxiv, xxxvi, 35, 54, 55, 68, 113, 118, 147

Field, 54, 55

   of Desire, 54, 55

first person, xix, xxix, 8, 10, 74, 101

forgive, 12, 116, 129

freedom, 8, 47, 52, 53, 65, 84

fundamental, 55, 74, 83

fundamentalist, xix, 6, 139

G

genes, xxi, 20, 21, 56, 66, 146, 148, 149

genius, xxi, 6, 20, 21, 26, 51, 56, 66, 68, 111, 133, 146, 149

gifts, xvii, xxi, 65, 146

Global, i, iii, xxxiii, xxxv, xxxvii, 61, 174, 175

   intimacy, xvi, xxv, xxvii, xxxii, xxxiii, xxxiv, xxxv, xxxvi, xxxvii, 7, 19, 23, 25, 34, 35, 48, 60, 61, 65, 66, 70, 77, 78, 79, 81, 84, 90, 93, 94, 95, 96, 102, 103, 104, 108, 112, 114, 118, 122, 126, 127, 130, 131, 132, 133, 139, 140, 141, 145

   intimacy disorder, xvi, xxxii, xxxiii, xxxiv, xxxv, xxxvi, xxxvii, 60, 61, 95, 104, 118

Global Action Paralysis, xxxv, 61

Goddess, 8, 37, 39, 49, 55, 76, 141
gorgeousness, 79
Gospel, 32, 96, 139, 140
ground, xii, xiii, xiv, xxviii, xxxviii, 60, 97, 98, 102, 173

H

habilis, 66
Hafiz, 9, 10, 36, 49, 101
Hallelujah, 2, 10, 37, 48, 49, 50, 68, 71, 92, 95, 96, 101, 102, 114, 115, 126, 135, 141, 153, 154
heart, xxvi, xxxviii, 1, 4, 14, 19, 20, 23, 25, 26, 30, 32, 37, 38, 39, 40, 48, 50, 54, 55, 56, 62, 63, 71, 82, 83, 97, 103, 109, 119, 123, 127, 128, 129, 130, 132, 144
heaven, 3, 42, 114, 137
Hebrew, 30, 32, 36, 38, 109, 129, 138, 140
hero, 93
Holy of Holies, xvi, 14, 35, 77, 101
Holy Trinity, 73, 125
Homo amor, xii, xx, 24, 25, 26, 27, 33, 41, 42, 45, 46, 47, 54, 62, 63, 64, 65, 66, 67, 68, 69, 70, 71, 90, 91, 92, 100, 108, 118, 119, 121, 124, 132, 133, 134, 140
Homo Deus, 33, 42, 46, 63, 64
Homo sapiens, xii, 23, 62, 69, 90, 108, 124, 133, 173
Homo sapiens sapiens, 90, 108, 124, 133
Homo universalis, 24, 66, 67
honor, 62, 67, 78, 90, 140
human, xvi, xx, xxvi, xxvii, xxviii, xxix, xxx, xxxi, xxxii, xxxiv, xxxvi, xxxviii, 8, 14, 15, 21, 24, 33, 34, 37, 41, 45, 51, 52, 62, 63, 64, 65, 66, 67, 69, 70, 82, 84, 85, 91, 93, 94, 100, 101, 107, 108, 109, 113, 118, 121, 130, 132, 133, 134, 137, 139, 144, 145, 148, 149, 173

humanism, xv, 41
humanity, xii, xv, xvii, xxi, xxix, xxx, 2, 21, 24, 31, 32, 43, 45, 53, 60, 64, 67, 69, 93, 107, 116, 117, 121, 132, 140, 142, 173, 174
humans, 52, 68, 115, 117, 133, 148, 149

I

identify, 44, 74
identity, xiv, xxxii, xxxiv, xxxv, xxxvi, xxxviii, 7, 90, 91, 95, 106, 123, 124, 140, 141, 173
illusion, 23, 97
imagination, 45, 74, 102, 126, 127
imagine, 13, 15, 30, 53, 54, 71, 102, 116, 147
immortality, 24, 33, 46, 63, 64, 66
impulse, xxvii, 8, 9, 10, 13, 14, 17, 22, 35, 49, 52, 69, 77, 92, 123, 131, 132, 133, 134, 147
individual, xiii, xxvi, xxxvi, 69, 79, 93, 96, 127
individuals, xxx, 54, 141, 149
infinite, xix, 12, 21, 33, 52, 102, 112, 125, 126, 141, 144, 145, 147
Infinite Personhood, 44, 49
Infinity of Intimacy, xix, xx, 6, 9, 10, 34, 35, 36, 37, 49, 50, 75, 92, 102, 112, 113, 114, 125, 126, 141
Infinity of Power, xix, 6, 9, 34, 49, 92, 101, 102
influence, xxv, 5, 25
Inside of the Inside, 14, 56, 77, 78, 101, 102
integrate, 119
integrating, xxxviii, 16
integration, 7, 46
integrity, xviii, 23, 104, 106
interior sciences, xiii, xx, xxvii, xxviii, xxxvii, xxxviii, 61, 92, 111, 112, 114
internet, xxx, 134
intimacy, xvi, xxv, xxvii, xxxii, xxxiii,

xxxiv, xxxv, xxxvi, xxxvii, 7, 19, 23, 25, 34, 35, 48, 60, 61, 65, 66, 70, 77, 78, 79, 81, 84, 90, 93, 94, 95, 96, 102, 103, 104, 108, 112, 114, 118, 122, 126, 127, 130, 131, 132, 133, 139, 140, 141, 145

intimate, xiv, xix, xxxiv, xxxv, xxxviii, 35, 60, 70, 78, 92, 96, 112, 118, 131, 133, 145

Intimate Universe, xx, xxxv, 35, 48, 70, 77, 78, 81, 112

irreducible, 66

Israel, 146

J

Jerusalem, 14

Jesus, 41, 116, 141

joining genes, xxi, 20, 21, 56, 146, 148

joining genius, xxi, 20, 26, 56, 133, 146, 149

joy, xii, xxiv, 7, 13, 22, 56, 63, 71, 104, 108, 134

K

Kabbalah, xvi, 138, 173

Kashmir Shaivism, xvi, 110

kehdabra, 84

kindness, 52

king, 153

kiss, 42

knowledge, xvi, 37, 38, 50, 51, 64, 90, 91, 92

L

larger whole, 7, 33, 38, 96, 97, 121

leadership, xi, 115

leading, xiv, xx, 64, 69, 89, 90, 103, 109, 121, 122, 123, 173

lev, 32

line, 78, 103

lo, 117

loneliness, 11, 12, 16, 18

longing, 115

Love, i, iii, iv, vi, xii, xviii, xx, xxi, xxiii, xxvi, xxxi, xxxv, xxxviii, 2, 7, 11, 24, 25, 26, 29, 31, 33, 37, 38, 41, 44, 45, 46, 47, 48, 49, 51, 52, 55, 59, 64, 65, 67, 68, 69, 75, 78, 79, 80, 81, 90, 91, 92, 93, 96, 97, 98, 99, 100, 101, 103, 104, 106, 108, 110, 111, 114, 115, 116, 118, 119, 123, 124, 135, 137, 138, 140, 141, 142, 143, 144, 145, 146, 148, 149, 152, 173

desire, xxxii, xxxviii, 4, 14, 19, 20, 23, 25, 26, 37, 38, 39, 48, 50, 52, 54, 55, 56, 63, 71, 81, 83, 84, 105, 112, 125, 126

story, xx, xxiv, xxxi, xxxii, xxxiii, xxxiv, xxxvi, xxxvii, xxxviii, 2, 7, 8, 14, 16, 21, 30, 32, 33, 34, 35, 36, 41, 42, 45, 46, 47, 53, 60, 61, 62, 66, 69, 71, 78, 79, 80, 83, 84, 89, 90, 91, 93, 94, 96, 98, 99, 100, 103, 108, 109, 110, 111, 112, 116, 121, 122, 123, 124, 134, 138, 139, 140, 141, 142, 143, 144, 145, 146, 147, 148, 149, 173, 174

Love Code, xviii, 37, 46, 75, 81

LoveIntelligence, xxv, 23, 25, 45, 65, 66, 100, 101, 108, 113, 123

Love Story, i, iii, iv, xx, xxxv, xxxviii, 48, 90, 93, 96, 99, 100, 123, 137, 138, 140, 148

M

ma, 31, 112

manifestation, 149

marriage, 38, 143

master, 35, 47

mathematics, 77, 78

meditation, 9, 36, 102, 113, 125, 140

memory, xxxv, xxxvii, 19, 20, 48, 55, 56

memory of the future, xxxv, 19, 48

metamorphosis, 38, 116, 117
metaphor, 49, 116, 126, 146
miracle, 27, 151
mitosis, 122
modern, xiv, xvi, xxvi, xxxiv, xxxvi,
        xxxviii, 7, 45, 46
Modernity, xxxi, xxxii
molecule, 141
mother, 76, 87
music, xviii, 77, 78, 79, 80, 153
mystery, xiv, 12, 46
mystic, 13, 35
mysticism, 5, 36, 38, 61
mythopoetic, 84, 101

N

New Age, 38, 70, 130, 132
new human, 21, 24, 41, 45, 64, 67, 100,
        107, 108, 118, 121, 132, 133,
        134, 149, 173
new humanity, xii, 21, 24, 45, 64, 67,
        107, 121, 140, 173
new Story, xi, xii, xiv, xv, xvi, xviii, xxi,
        xxiii, xxiv, xxx, xxxi, xxxvii,
        xxxviii, 111
noosphere, 25, 62, 134

O

obligation, 108, 134, 140
    of consciousness, xvi, xix, xxii, xxiv,
        xxviii, 3, 5, 11, 12, 13, 17, 22, 23,
        26, 50, 97, 101, 107, 121, 174
Eye, xvii, xxi, xxix, xxx, 2, 24, 31, 53,
        60, 69, 116, 117, 132, 142, 174
    of intimacy, xxv, xxvii, xxxiii, xxxv,
        xxxvi, xxxvii, 7, 25, 34, 35, 48,
        61, 65, 66, 77, 78, 81, 84, 93, 94,
        95, 96, 103, 104, 108, 112, 114,
        118, 122, 126, 127, 130, 133,
        140, 145
    of love, xxiii, xxiv, xxv, xxvi, xxxvii,
        xxxviii, 42, 43, 44, 45, 46, 62, 65,

        79, 89, 91, 96, 98, 99, 100, 107,
        108, 109, 117, 121, 123, 124,
        126, 130, 139, 140, 145, 146, 147
ontological, xxviii, 110
otherness, xxxiv, xxxv, 140, 141
Outrageous Act of Love, 55
Outrageous Acts of Love, 48, 55, 100,
        123, 124
Outrageous Love, xii, xviii, xx, xxvi,
        xxxviii, 7, 24, 31, 44, 48, 49, 55,
        75, 78, 97, 98, 99, 100, 101, 104,
        106, 118, 119, 123, 135, 140, 145
Outrageous Love Story, xxxviii, 99,
        100, 123

P

particles, xxxvi, 8, 83, 140, 145
particular, xxvii, 15, 44, 64, 68, 85, 90,
        91, 95, 106, 107, 129, 130, 139,
        145, 146
pathology, 20
pathos, xxxv, 141
Personhood of Cosmos, xix, 49
Pesach, 38
pleasure, 73, 105
plotline, 91, 122
power, xvii, xxvii, xxxii, xxxviii, 7, 14,
        34, 45, 52, 66, 82, 112, 116, 117,
        130, 147, 148
prayer, xviii, xix, 2, 4, 5, 6, 9, 21, 25,
        26, 36, 37, 48, 50, 51, 76, 92, 98,
        101, 112, 113, 124, 125, 131, 141
prehension, 83, 105
promise, 15, 16, 98, 123, 143
proto-touch, 83
Psalms, 76
pseudo-eros, xvi, 20, 91
psychology, xxvi
Purim, 30
purpose, xxxiv, xxxv, 46, 141

Q

quantum, 83, 115, 148, 174

R

raba, 109
radical, xxvii, 6, 15, 16, 17, 23, 47, 56,
    81, 83, 102, 104, 105, 107, 109,
    141
ratzuf, 35, 47, 77, 92, 100
Reality, xiii, xvi, xix, xx, xxiv, xxvii,
    xxxii, xxxiv, xxxvi, xxxvii,
    xxxviii, 6, 7, 19, 22, 32, 33, 41,
    43, 44, 47, 48, 55, 65, 70, 74, 83,
    85, 90, 93, 94, 95, 96, 97, 98, 99,
    100, 101, 102, 104, 105, 106,
    108, 109, 110, 111, 112, 113,
    122, 123, 124, 125, 126, 130,
    137, 139, 141, 144, 145, 146
realization, xiii, xvi, xix, xx, xxvii, xx-
    viii, xxix, xxxvii, 21, 36, 45, 69,
    100, 101, 114, 121, 122, 126, 139
reclaiming, xix, 33, 73, 124
reflect, xxi, 139
relationship, 91, 94, 143
religion, xxxi, xxxviii, 34, 49, 60, 69,
    80, 81, 101, 110, 112, 141, 173
Renaissance, xxiii, xxx, 7, 45, 79, 80,
    138
resonance, xxxiii, 2, 31, 128
resurrection, 32, 40, 41, 42, 70, 116,
    117
revealed, 78, 131
revelation, xxxi, xxxii, 132, 140
role mate, 20, 21
Rumi, xxv, 8, 9, 34, 36, 49, 75, 81, 101

S

sacred, 77, 97, 100
sappir, 140
second person, 10, 75
second shock of existence, xxviii, xxix,
    xxx, 68, 69
security, 101

Seder, 32, 38, 39
Self, xii, xv, xvi, xx, xxi, xxvii, 17, 30,
    62, 63, 65, 66, 80, 90, 95, 100,
    103, 123, 124, 134, 139, 144,
    146, 154, 173
  organized, 134
  organizing, 31, 65, 71, 117, 118, 124,
    134, 135
separate self, 62, 83, 84, 90
separation, 23
sexual, 11, 19, 21, 82, 85, 86, 133, 134
sexuality, 21, 148, 149
shame, 130
social construction, 7
Solomon, xvi, xx, 14, 35, 47, 64, 75, 77,
    92, 100, 119
Song of Songs, 18, 47, 49
soul mate, 20, 21
source code, xvi, xxii, xxiv, 43, 44, 48,
    62, 80, 90, 95, 98, 103, 134, 142,
    173, 174
spirituality, xx, 67, 68, 173
story, xx, xxiv, xxxi, xxxii, xxxiii, xxxiv,
    xxxvi, xxxvii, xxxviii, 2, 7, 8, 14,
    16, 21, 30, 32, 33, 34, 35, 36, 41,
    42, 45, 46, 47, 53, 60, 61, 62, 66,
    69, 71, 78, 79, 80, 83, 84, 89, 90,
    91, 93, 94, 96, 98, 99, 100, 103,
    108, 109, 110, 111, 112, 116,
    121, 122, 123, 124, 134, 138,
    139, 140, 141, 142, 143, 144,
    145, 146, 147, 148, 149, 173, 174
structures, 85, 94, 108, 132
Sufism, xxv, 79
suicide, 61, 63
synagogue, 6, 73, 75, 77, 110, 118

T

Talmud, 31
temple, 77
tenderness, 102, 125, 126
Thanos, 93
the One, xii, xix, xxv, 33, 38, 41, 52,

73, 75, 79, 80, 96, 103, 110, 114, 119, 141
the Universe, 65, 90, 93, 96, 99, 100, 124, 138, 148
The Universe, 123
  A Love Story, 48, 90, 93, 96, 99, 100, 123, 137, 138, 140, 148
third person, xix, 8, 74, 75, 101
Thou Art That, 8, 74
traditions, xii, xiii, xvi, xx, 5, 31, 33, 38, 60, 61, 100
tragic, xii, 33, 61, 85, 109
transfiguration, 69
transformation, xiv, xv, xxvii, 14, 15, 31, 33, 39, 42, 44, 65, 117, 139
transmission, xv, xvii, xviii, 123
True Self, 62
truth, xxiv, xxvi, xxxviii, 7, 80, 81, 83, 101, 104, 137, 151, 154

U

uncertainty, 36, 46, 127
understanding, xvii, 67, 68, 108, 145
unique gift, 25, 49, 51, 65, 122
uniqueness, xiv, 51, 133, 149
unique risk, 100, 106, 122
Unique Self, xii, xv, xvi, xx, xxi, 17, 30, 62, 63, 65, 66, 80, 90, 95, 100, 103, 123, 124, 134, 139, 144, 146, 173
Unique Self Symphony, xvi, 63, 65, 66, 90, 95, 100, 103, 123, 124, 134, 139, 146
Universe, xiii, xiv, xx, xxviii, xxxi, xxxii, xxxv, 35, 48, 65, 70, 74, 77, 78, 81, 90, 91, 93, 96, 99, 100, 109, 112, 123, 124, 138, 148
  A Love Story, i, iii, iv, xxxv, 48, 90, 93, 96, 99, 100, 123, 137, 138, 140, 148
Universe Story, xiv, xxxi, xxxii, 91
unmanifest, 6, 19, 145
Upanishads, 74

utopia, xxx, 7, 41, 43, 80, 92, 106, 107, 109, 137, 141, 146

V

Vajrayana, 110
values, xii, xiii, xxxii, xxxiii, xxxvi, xxxvii, 45
visionary, 5, 26, 173
vital, xv, xvii, xviii, 18, 130
vocation, 68

W

wake, xxxvi, 3, 52, 59, 65
Walden, 35
WeSpace, 95
Western, 64
Wheel of Co-Creation, 19, 174
where we are, 41, 61
whole mate, 20, 21, 29, 47, 59, 107, 122, 134
who we are, 45, 63, 131

Y

yarmulke, 143
yearning, 19, 20, 35, 112, 115
Yom Kippur, 129

Z

Zohar, 74

ABOUT THE AUTHORS

Dr. Marc Gafni is a visionary world philosopher and futurist, one of the leading formulators of world spirituality and religion of our time, and a beloved teacher and public intellectual. He holds his doctorate in philosophy from Oxford University, as well as Orthodox rabbinic ordination. He co-founded the activist think tank, now called the Center for World Philosophy and Religion where he serves as the co-president with Dr. Zachary Stein. He also served with Barbara Marx Hubbard as co-president of the Foundation for Conscious Evolution, which he consented to lead at Barbara's request after her passing.

He is known for his "source code teachings"—including Unique Self theory and the Five Selves, the Amorous Cosmos, a Politics of Evolutionary Love, a Return to Eros, and Digital Intimacy—and has more than twenty books to his name, including the award-winning Your Unique Self, A Return to Eros, and three volumes of Radical Kabbalah.

He teaches on the cutting edge of philosophy in the West, helping to evolve a new "*dharma*" or meta-theory of Integral meaning that is helping to re-shape key pivoting points in global consciousness and culture, with the aim of participating in the articulation of what Dr. Gafni together with Dr. Stein and colleagues are calling CosmoErotic Humanism.

At the core of CosmoErotic Humanism is what Dr. Gafni and Dr. Stein are calling First Principles and First Values, Anthro-Ontology, and a Universal Grammar of Value. This is the ground of a new shared universe story and a new narrative of identity for the new human and the new humanity. This is what they are calling the emergence from Homo sapiens to Homo Amor.

This shared story rooted in First Principles and First Values can then serve as the matrix for a global ethos for a global civilization.

Together with Dr. Stein and Ken Wilber, Gafni is writing a series of seminal books under the collective pseudonym of David J. Temple, which intend to evolve the source code of consciousness and culture in response to the meta-crisis. The first of those books is *First Principles and First Values: Forty-Two Propositions on CosmoErotic Humanism, the Meta-Crisis, and the World to Come.*

Barbara Marx Hubbard (born Barbara Marx; December 22, 1929–April 10, 2019) was an American futurist, author, and public speaker. She is credited with the Wheel of Co-Creation and together with Dr. Gafni, the Wheel of Co-Creation 2.0, as well as the concepts of the Synergy Engine and the "birthing" of humanity.

As co-founder and president of the Foundation for Conscious Evolution and the chair, for the last five years of her life, of the Center for World Philosophy and Religion, she posited that humanity was on the threshold of a quantum leap if newly emergent scientific, social, and spiritual capacities were integrated to address global crises.

She was the author of seven books on social and planetary evolution. In conjunction with the Shift Network, she co-produced the worldwide "Birth 2012" multimedia event. She was also the subject of a biography by author Neale Donald Walsch, *The Mother of Invention: The Legacy of Barbara Marx Hubbard.* Deepak Chopra called her "the voice for conscious evolution."

In 1984, she was symbolically nominated for the vice presidency of the United States. She also co-chaired a number of Soviet-American Citizen Summits, introducing a new concept called SYNCON, to foster synergistic convergence with opposing groups. In addition, she co-founded the World Future Society and the Association for Global New Thought.

Volume 14 — Conscious Evolution: A Love Story

LIST OF EPISODES

1. Episode 131 — April 13, 2019
2. Episode 132 — April 20, 2019
3. Episode 133 — April 27, 2019
4. Episode 134 — May 5, 2019
5. Episode 135 — May 11, 2019
6. Episode 136 — May 18, 2019
7. Episode 137 — May 25, 2019
8. Episode 138 — June 1, 2019
9. Episode 139 — June 8, 2019
10. Episode 140 — June 15, 2019